DIDN'T YOU READ MY BOOK?

Dr. Richard E. Eby

Treasure House

a division of
Destiny Image
P.O. Box 310
Shippensburg, PA 17257-0310

ISBN 1-56043-448-1

For Worldwide Distribution
Printed in the U.S.A.

First Printing:	1991
Second Printing:	1992
Third Printing:	1992
Fourth Printing:	1993
Fifth Printing:	1993

Destiny Image books are available through these fine distributors outside the United States:

Christian Growth, Inc.,
Jalan Kilang-Timor, Singapore 0315

Successful Christian Living
Capetown, Rep. of South Africa

Lifestream
Nottingham, England

Vision Resources
Ponsonby, Auckland, New Zealand

Rhema Ministries Trading
Randburg, South Africa

WA Buchanan Company
Geebung, Queensland, Australia

Salvation Book Centre
Petaling, Jaya, Malaysia

Word Alive
Niverville, Manitoba, Canada

WHY READ HIS BOOK? GOD'S WRITTEN WORD HIS SCRIPTURES, THE HOLY BIBLE

1. *God's Own Book* recounts His observations of *mankind's* faltering journey from a new garden in Eden to a new Heaven and earth. It is the *only* account that the eternal Eyewitness on Heaven's throne has put in writing for His chosen peoples' research and understanding.

2. *God's Book* is *His* Word, *His* revelation. In It *His* prophesies become fulfillments; His promises become experiences; *His* chastenings produce perfections; *His* words become living creations in surrendered lives.

3. *God's Book* says His love is relentless, His judgments non-compromising, His mercy overriding, His throne approachable, His sovereignty unassailable, His spirit available, and His Son invincible.

4. *God's Book* is His proffered *guideline*: His Son is His *lifeline*: and His spirit is His *prayerline*. To His willing followers He gives them all as *His gift* of life!

5. *God's Book* reveals that He is truly one, the same yesterday, today and forever, the Most High God who alone can create! The Book also reveals Him as an Ever-Adapting Administrator with limitless resourcefulness to meet the ever-changing needs of His human family on earth.

6. *God's Book* is *authoritative* about man's need of salvation on earth and a home in Heaven with Him. His warning words are His denunciations of sin, Satan, and hell. "The Book" permits *no middle ground*: Yeshua saves lives; Satan destroys them. God keeps asking...

"Didn't You Read My Book?"

WHY BELIEVE HIS SON? GOD'S LIVING WORD JESUS, YESHUA

1. YESHUA as the *Anointed Son* of the Most High God is the one Sovereign Lord who died, arose, and reigns as *our Advocate* at the right hand of the Father, in Heaven's Throne Room. Nothing written about Him can fully convey or explain the totality of His love, mercy or Divine goodness.

2. YESHUA as *Savior* is limitless in His persistence and methods of seeking lost, dying souls in order to rescue them from Hell. He was given the Only Name under Heaven with *that power!*

3. YESHUA as *Teacher* never tires of imparting His knowledge and truths, at any time, manner or means befitting the searching minds of earthly creatures who seek Him *from the heart.*

4. YESHUA as the *Head* of His *Body* the Church is its Life, its Provider and Protector, its Doctor and Director. His mind, strength and wisdom become inseparable from

His Body at the Rapture. Heaven is His Home (and theirs) wherein is Eternal Life!

5. YESHUA as *King of Kings* has already established His *heavenly* Kingdom of God. He will soon establish His Davidic Kingdom here to rule the nations, once Satan is bound. *By grace*, present-day believers in Jesus are given His gift of citizenship in Heaven. As Messiah, He will join "lost" Israel to Judah as His "spotless" Bride.

6. YESHUA as the *Alpha and Omega* of the total creation calls Himself God's AMEN, the "I AM" of all that there is, anytime and anywhere. As such He claims His title as the Lamb of God which taketh away the sins of the world! Hallelujah!

   YESHUA said, "It's *all* in My Book!"

Note: During His disscussions with me YESHUA the Messiah of the Old Covenant, known as Jesus the Christ in the New Covenant, validated the Sacred Scriptures (writings) as "My Book."

PREFACE

(Note to Hebrew, Samaritan, and Gentile readers: the NAME above all names is "Yeshua" in Hebrew, "Jesus" in Greek, Latin or English).

To help you validate my autobiography involving the loving care of Yeshua for His earthly family, this book includes marginal Scriptural references which augment and parallel my accounts of encounters with Messiah. It is far *more important* for a reader to *study* inerrant truths from the Bible, God's Book, than merely to read about the author's conversations with Him, no matter how exciting or edifying they may be. Jesus told me, "Everything you need to know is the The Book!"

Fallen Satan today is having a hey-day discounting both old and new testimonies about YESHUA! Even from (some) pulpits today he sneers at doctrines which lift up the Name YESHUA, Whom he hates with a frenzy like a roaring lion! He hates the Bible with a passion! It is the only *accurate* record of God's (G-d's) declarations to mankind which expose satan for who he is, what he does, and where he will end up! Satan hates the *Bible* for revealing that any man can *avoid* Hell by choosing Yeshua as Messiah and Lord instead of blindly following a born-loser, Satan, whose *empty* promises end in a lake of eternal fire.

I share the following *experiences* from a lifetime on an exciting path with my Savior in the fervent prayer that they will lead each reader to "search all *Scriptures*" more frequently and fervently. They were written for our inspiration, edification, and understanding of *the* revelations of Truth. This little book can motivate you to seek and enjoy a closer relationship with God, Son, and Spirit, so that we can intensify *our* spiritual warfare against our deadly enemy, Satan.

Praise be to God! As partakers of God's unsearchable Heavenly riches we can already walk and talk with Him *here* and *now*!

Dr. Richard E. Eby

Contents

INTRODUCTION

BEFORE I KNEW HIM, JESUS LOVED ME

This partial autobiography can only be told because YESHUA loved me long before I could know Him![1]

He arranged these special encounters between us. In *no way* could I have merited any such personal attention from my Creator! Through *His* grace alone He had been wanting me to be an eyewitness and a reporter of *"the things which God hath prepared for them that love Him."* His expressed purpose has been that I share them *and Him* with you, in fact, to "shout" that *He* is God![2]

Only because my Lord commanded me to "Tell them, Tell them, Tell them" do I feel secure in relating our encounters which have been so personal and unbelievingly exciting. In advance of my writing these miraculous events, Yeshua had already placed parallel accounts in His own Book to which I have made marginal references in this one.[3]

Background Data

As an introduction to this series of conversations with my Savior Jesus Christ a bit of background will afford an appropriate setting. The earthly part of this account naturally started with my parents...[4]

Mother Told Me About Her First Amazing Miracle

An eleven year old girl (who was to be my future mother) had stumbled homeward one day from her one-room school-house in Michigan, semi-conscious. In a few hours she was dead. That evening her friend, the Patawatomi Chieftain, had ridden into the farmyard as her grieving father returned home with the newly made coffin tied to his mare's saddle. Abruptly, the Chief had announced: "My Great White Spirit tells me that Little Girl will live if you let me cover her with sacred medicine. She wake up in morning, drink water at noon, then walk at sundown." Grampa prayerfully agreed, and the black goo-ish concoction was applied to the corpse! At sunrise her body came alive![5]

(A few years before this, Grampa had become the favored friend of the Chief after telling him about the Heavenly Father's love. The Chief had accepted Yeshua as his Lord.)

Her second miracle was to be me years later. As a beautiful young wife she had discovered that her temporary death had left her barren (the doctors reported "withered organs—no explanation"). Undaunted, she had repeated Hannah's prayer, in total faith that her loving Lord would (like Hannah's answer) give her a man-child to be dedicated to Him even before birth! And so it happened.[6]

Her third miracle occurred at her sixth month of pregnancy. She suddenly miscarried a dead fetus which the obstetrician laid aside to await the autopsy later that night. When he returned and unwrapped the hospital towel, the form started breathing. In panic, he ordered the mother (with a shoe box containing the gasping infant) to go home. Once there, she besought her Lord to instruct her *daily* as to how to care for this baby! He did. I am His living proof today![7]

My past seventy-eight years are now history. I grew up in the tender, loving home of Christian parents. Our home was Jesus' home too. He was our unseen Guest, a very present help in times of trouble, just as His Book had promised! This youngster assumed that all little boys were being raised to share and shed God's love upon others. It seemed so sensible to let our "Big Friend" in Heaven love us all.[8]

Then I learned about the devil who hated my God, told lies, led an army of demons against God's friends, and ended up "getting almost everyone dead." In 1972, he proved his intent for me when he arranged that I would die suddenly from a fall on my head off a balcony in Chicago. (The details have been told already in my first two books, *Caught Up Into Paradise*, and *Tell Them I Am Coming*.)[9]

Jesus was watching my fall that day. He decided to teach Satan *again* that our Creator is also the Resurrection and the Life. He caught me instantly up to Paradise to show me Glory! It was a life-bestowing experience *with* Him, so important that He told me to share it with you.[10]

So I must! He left my dead, bloodless body in a Chicago backyard, and *I* was at the same instant in Paradise, that place which Jesus promised to prepare for believers when He died for us.[11]

I gasped! Suddenly in a new body in a new place with new life, I was ecstaticly joyful: no pain, no tears, no sorrow, no memory. Nothing but incomprehensible peace and infilling love. All was perfection. I stood awestruck in a new weightless body, translucent and floating. Total love enveloped and perfused me! What peace![12]

Then THE VOICE: unmistakably sovereign, majestic, Divine! None other can ever compare. It seemed to originate within my head, speaking from me, yet to me. With the authority of God It thundered across a great valley in which I had just landed:

"Dick, You're Dead!"

The Voice of my Creator was speaking! It explained how I had gotten to Heaven in timeless speed; and above all It established an intimacy between us which is called Divine Love. I was *His* child, Dick! Never had I been more excited. Truly I was in Heaven's Paradise, *in* Jesus, with His mind *in* me. We were as one![14]

I invite each reader to share with me the following descriptions of how Jesus spoke with me in Paradise, in Hell, on earth, and through His Book. He specifically commanded me to tell such things, saying: "These are the last days before I return for My Body of Believers (the Church*). I am coming for them soon!" He explained that He would be giving some of His children (when "available") many documenting evidences to validate His prophecies. "I need eyewitnesses of My Glory and Truth *now*. You are but one. Go, tell them, tell them, tell them! There is but a little while until I come for My Body of Believers."[15]

Each time that I asked Him a question, he posed His own in response:

"DIDN'T YOU READ MY BOOK?"

That is His challenge to every reader.

*Note: Not once did Yeshua (Jesus) use our word "church" as meaning a denominational building: only a "called-out group" of faithful believers called by Him "saints".

END NOTES

1. Ps. 139:14-18   **2**. John 15:16; Matt. 10:27; Isa. 45:5-8   **3**. Matt. 13:35; John 15:11   **4**. John 16:13-15   **5**. John 10:4   **6**. I Sam. 1:11,20; Ps. 113:9; Ps. 139:13-16   **7**. Jer. 1:5; Ps. 22:9-10; John 14:13; Ps. 46:1   **8**. Heb. 13:5; Rev. 3:20; Ps. 46:1; I Pet. 4:10   **9**. John 8:44; I Pet. 5:8-9 **10**. Heb. 4:13-14; John 11:25 **11**. John 14:3 **12**. I Cor. 15:54; Rom. 5:8 **13**. Rev. 14:2 **14**. II Cor. 5:8; John 17:20-24 **15**. Matt. 28:19-20; Col. 1:18; Eph. 1:23; I Thess. 4:15

PART ONE
PERSONAL DIALOGUES WITH JESUS IN HEAVEN

Question #1
"JESUS, WHERE AM I?"

My earthly life on that July Day in 1972 was instantly interrupted by a *blaze of unearthly light*, by instant immersion in total peace, and by a nearly *deafening* Voice:

"DICK, YOU'RE DEAD!"[1]

Imagine my dilemma: I land from somewhere on my feet, suddenly, with a sharp thud, in a *new* body, amidst unfamiliar foliage, and with a mind which heard The Voice speaking inside my head! It was so indescribable.[2]

Then to have *no* memory (of where I had come from, how I had gotten there, or why I was still "me" with a brand *new body and mind*) left me awed. Unbelievable![3]

To see without my glasses a long valley filled with perfect horticultural specimens quietly emitting their appropriate colors; to hear heavenly music surrounding me, then to sense a permeating aroma of exquisite fragrance—it all seemed impossibly ecstatic![4]

I gasped. The new body was painless, seemingly made of "abundant joy." I discovered that it reacted instantly to anything I thought—no delays. The mind had no sense of fear: instead, a total peace despite the newness and suddenness of landing there. I was more alive and awake in that glowing body than seemed possible.[5]

Everything was bathed in shadowless light, with a baptism of love. Then it hit me! I WAS AT HOME! MY REAL HOME! I BELONGED HERE where the presence of Jesus enfolded me.[6]

I was momentarily speechless with the ecstasy of it all! Then I realized that Jesus' Voice had declared me "dead." Yet *I* was totally alive. (He really had meant that only the former body and its imperfect mind were dead). A glance down the gorgeous length of my valley ended my silence: I heard my self shout:

"JESUS, WHERE AM I?"[7]

Instantly, before I could complete my query, that same Voice in a tone of gentle thunder echoed within my head:

"DIDN'T YOU READ MY BOOK?"[8]

He was speaking to me (in fact, *in* me) with a speed greater than lightning, and in a language of sweet purity unlike anything that an earthly tongue could utter. I gasped again. I had HIS MIND, impossible as it seemed! Every word clearly meant exactly what was being said. We seemed to have a joint mind: I would ask, and He would answer. (The speed of this communication in such a MIND is hard to describe in human terms. Perchance I can now liken it to a printed page on which the questions being typed have the answers typed upon them, line upon line, at the same time, instantly.)[9]

Yeshua began His answer: "If you had read My Book you would have *known* all the answers. Before I ever told My disciples to preach My Good News, I promised never to leave nor forsake them. As I sat outside the Temple I disclosed my impending death *and* My return to Glory as being necessary for their ministry. *Then* I would transfer my Power to them by sending My Holy Spirit *into* them from Pentecost onward. He would take My place in and among them on earth as another Comforter! I gave them a certain promise:[10]

'I am going to prepare a *place* for you. I will come again and receive you unto Myself, that where I am there may ye be also.'[11]

"I had already explained to my followers that My Father had made them one *in* Me, as I was one *in* the Father. That makes us inseparable, as ONE." Jesus paused as though the next thought on His Mind pained Him greatly.[12]

"My son," He resumed, "as is written in My Book, on the next day I was arrested, tried, and crucified for claiming identity with Jehovah. At My right hung a dying thief who stopped ridiculing Me when he noted the sign over My head: 'KING OF THE JEWS.' He *believed* it when he looked into My eyes, and called over to Me: 'Master, remember Thou me when You come into Your Glory!'

"My Book tells you that I immediately promised him: '*This day shalt thou be with Me in Paradise!*'[13]

"The thief heard me before the centurions broke his legs so he would die immediately! My beloved disciples, John, also heard Me as he stood near My bleeding feet. I then asked him to take My mother home with him because he could explain what I had said to her and the disciples.[14]

"I gave up My Spirit to My Father as soon as I announced to the crowd, '*It is finished!*' *Then I was free to prepare Paradise for that repentant thief in Heaven.* This is My Home here in the Third Heaven with My saints. You are in Paradise this day!"[15]

Jesus had answered my first question! I had instantly sensed that I was *in Heaven* upon arrival there; but now I knew *which part* this was! I had so much more to ask about this new Home.[16]

END NOTES

1. II Cor. 12:1-4; Rev. 21:23; John 12:29 **2.** I Cor. 15:44,50 **3.** Rom. 11:34 **4.** Isa. 25:8 **5.** Eph. 4:23; John 14:27 **6.** Phil. 3:20; II Cor. 5:2 **7.** Matt. 22:32; Luke 20:38; John 11:25 **8.** Job 40:9; Luke 24:25-27 **9.** II Tim. 3:15-17; I Cor. 2:16 **10.** Matt. 22:40; Luke 1:70; 24:27; Luke 24:47; Heb. 13:5; Acts 1:8; Luke 24:49; John 14:16,26 **11.** John 14:3 **12.** John 14:20; John 14:10 **13.** Luke 23:39-43; Luke 23:42-43 **14.** John 19:32; John 19:27 **15.** John 10:17-18; John 19:28; Matt. 5:16; Matt. 6:9 **16.** II Cor. 12:2-4; Rev. 4:1-2

Question #2

"LORD, WHAT IS PARADISE?"

To be talking with the Creator of the Universe, mind to mind, *in* this Paradise, was unspeakably exciting. Questions flooded through my new mind.[1]

"But Jesus," I blurted out, "Tell me Your *definition* of Paradise. It is obvious that I am in Heaven with You because everything is so perfect. Tell me more!"

As He replied, His regal voice seemed to bubble over with excitement and joy and love. I sensed His pleasure at having a child of His come home this day:[2]

"My child, didn't you read My Book? I was so careful to explain that *I* would prepare for each of you *in* the *heavenly places*, an abode with Me. I even arranged for my disciples to watch Me ascend into the heavens, enfolded in My Shekinah Glory cloud. I assigned two angels to meet them there outside of Bethany to reassure them that I would return in like manner. And I will do so![3]

"Later I allowed My chosen lad, Stephen, to see Me seated at the right hand of My Father in Heaven, just to prove to his executioners that I was there, alive! Saul had ordered the stoning. He was holding Stephen's clothes. It shocked him to hear Stephen shout with ecstasy at seeing Me. You see, I had plans for Saul that would require Me to blind him with My Light and later be stoned to death at Lystra so I could catch *him* up to this Third Heaven and show *him* the *unspeakable glories* of Heaven. He would be instantly persuaded from then on that *absolutely nothing* could ever separate him from Our love. After he saw Paradise, I told him to write about it, and I changed his name to Paul."[4]

As Jesus talked, I became increasingly startled. The speed of His "heaven-language" was incredible yet totally clear within my head. At the same instant He was obviously replacing the needed memories which death of my original brain tissue had erased. Later, as we walked and talked that day I discovered that He also placed upon my new mind the very questions which I should ask! Only by asking Him the *proper question* could He give the *needed answer!*[5]

(After He returned me to life on earth I checked His Book to find confirmation of this truth: sure enough, there it is: Jesus' earthly brother James had written to us: "Ye ask and receive not because *ye ask amiss.*" Also, St. Paul nailed down the fact by writing: "…We know not what we should pray for as we ought…but the *Spirit* itself makes *intercession for us.*" What a lesson for us on earth! *For us* the Spirit prays, and *for us* Jesus looks upon the heart to find our true need!)[6]

"A Holding Tank"

"Now, My son, to answer your question: Paradise is a *holding tank* for the souls who have accepted Me as their Savior simply by *faith* in My having laid down My life to redeem them from the curse of sin. I prepared a new place for each of them, as I had promised. It is one of My gifts of mercy and grace, that their *joy* may be full! Here they become one with Me, completing the talents which I gave each one so that each can function as a distinct member in My Body.[7]

"Paradise is also *My Heavenly school* for perfecting the saints. You must be *taught* how to become priests and kings in My Kingdom so as to teach others to worship My Father in *spirit* and in *truth. I am your Teacher* renewing your mind to comprehend the greatness of our *unsearchable riches* of grace and mercy and love for all."[8]

He paused from His exciting explanation to let me gasp.

Another query burst from my mind to His: "Do You mean, Jesus, that each of Your children in Paradise has a separate place just for his particular enjoyment?"[9]

"Yes, My Son! Didn't you read in My Book that I would go to prepare a PLACE—not a commune, nor a kibutz; not a tenement nor a tract house? It would be a place fit for providing the abundant joys and fulfilled dreams and talents of each child, as a *new* creature, My *joint* heir! Each person is unlike any other, except that I am *in* each one, perfecting, teaching, sanctifying. Each of their abodes reflects the perfection of the purposes and promises for which I prepare My people and places!"[10]

"I know My sheep, just as *they know* My Voice. I made them. Heaven is so large that I have unlimited space for each one's paradise, a place of his own. This is just a tiny portion of Heaven. I have limitless plans. *I* think of Paradise as My sheepfold; I am its gate!"[11]

"This is *your* paradise. It is what you could not fashion for yourself, so I did it for you. That was my promise. It is your *temporary* abode for now!"[12]

I was stunned with excitement. This huge valley of celestial beauty was mine? The perfection of its forests, flowers, meadows and mountains was awesome.

But even so, the Presence of Jesus in and about me was more important right now. I must ask another question that suddenly formed.[13]

END NOTES

1. Deut. 5:24; Ps. 145:5-6 **2.** Ps. 147:11; Rev. 12:12a; John 4:36 **3.** John 14:2-3; Rev. 2:7; Luke 24:51; Acts 1:9-11; Rev. 22:20 **4.** Acts 7:55-56; Acts 9:3-6; Acts 14:19; II Cor. 12:2-4; Rom. 8:38-39 **5.** Amos 4:13; Ps. 139:2 **6.** James 4:3; Rom. 8:26-27; Luke 5:22; Luke 9:47; Luke 12:17,20 **7.** John 10:11; Rev. 4:1-2; John 15:11; Rom. 12:4-6 **8.** Eph. 4:12; Rev. 1:6; John 4:21-24; Heb. 5:12; Mark 6:34; Eph. 4:23-24 **9.** John 14:3 **10.** II Cor. 4:14-15; Rom. 8:17; II Cor. 5:17; John 17:21; I Cor. 7:7 **11.** John 10:14; John 10:4,27; John 10:9 **12.** Isa. 64:4; Ps. 23:6; Ps. 4:8 **13.** II Cor. 5:8

Question #3

"A TEMPORARY PLACE...?"

Surely this great valley (among whose meadows of flowers I found myself standing) looked to be permanent. Yet Jesus had stated that it was a *temporary* abode, a holding tank! Four-petalled flowers with their golden throats extended up into my legs, apparently as oblivious of my presence, as I was insensitive to theirs. Nothing seemed at all temporary.

In amazement I asked, "Jesus, what is *temporary* about this place, my paradise? It seems timeless to me!"[1]

"Didn't you read My Book, son? My Father's plans are even greater for you than this. I explained that He is preparing a Body of new creatures, which I have called *members*. This is the place where the souls of you who die *before* that BODY is completed are being assembled. Each member has an assignment to perform once I join him to Me, The Head. Each day more members are being added as My earthly children surrender themselves into My arms. One of these days My Body of true believers will be completed to My Father's satisfaction." He paused as though the joy of that thought had overwhelmed Him for the moment.[2]

"My Father assures Me that the time is yet a little while, but *very little*. Soon He will call those already in Paradise to surround Me as we descend from this third Heaven to the first

Heaven around the Earth. The souls of all My saints will be instantly clothed in their new resurrection bodies, as will the living saints on earth who rise to us in the Glory Cloud! At the sounding Trumpet they all receive new bodies and rise to meet us in the air. We return as *My Body* to My Throne Room with the Father. Now do you understand why I called this place a temporary abiding place? Do you grasp what it will mean to be one with Me and the Father in your incorruptible bodies? My Book states that I assumed mankind's sin so you 'might be made the Righteousness of God' *in* me!"[3]

I can clearly recall how Jesus' Voice paused at this moment. He was savouring an anticipation too intense and private to be revealed. Was He pre-living that moment at which He would enjoy the victory which His Father would give Him as the eternal reward for His own *long-suffering*? His own sting of death would be swallowed up, and He would be the Omniscient *Head* of a *completed* and *compliant Body* for whom He had shed His blood on a terrible Cross. He would reign as KING of the Jews after these days of Grace. Then His thoughts returned to me.[4]

"My son, when that time has come, My Father will call to Me. The applause of the heavenly hosts will be deafening; they too have been awaiting that day, ever since they announced my birth to the shepherds at Bethlehem so long ago. *Scoffers* will gaze with fear and wonder as My angelic hosts watch Me fulfill My promise to My *earthly* Body of *believers* at My soon return to Earth.[5]

"My Book records the *many signs* which will precede My coming for My Family. I tried to explain those events to My disciples, very carefully. I promised them that I was leaving My Holy Spirit as a Comforter to instruct them as they studied My Word, and to tell them of the *things to come*. I want My children to be informed about Our plans in advance. I want them to be filled with My *joy*. After all, they are mine: I created them and bought them back from satanic slavery. I told them that I would come for them so that we could be together forever. My Father wants them *all* to believe *Me*."[6]

His lightening-fast discourse ceased. I surveyed my paradise and this new body that floated![7]

END NOTES

1. John 13:36 **2.** Gal. 6:15; II Cor. 5:17; Rom. 12:5-8; Eph. 5:23; Acts 2:41, 5:14; Acts 11:24; Rom. 8:21 **3.** John 16:16-22; Heb. 10:37: Jude 14; I Thess. 3:13; I Cor. 15:51-54; II Cor. 5:1-9; I Thess. 4:17; John 14:20; II Cor. 5:21 **4.** II Pet. 3:9,15; I Tim. 1:16; I Cor. 15:55; Eph. 5:30,32; Hos. 6:1-3; II Pet. 3:8 **5.** I Thess. 4:13-18; Luke 2:13,14; II Pet. 3:3-4; Luke 12:45-46; Acts 1:10-11; Hos. 2:14,19,20 **6.** Isa. 42:9; Jer. 31:1,3; Matt. 24:3-8; John 14:26; John 15:26; Luke 12:12; John 16:13; John 16:24; II Pet. 3:8-9

Question #4
"ETERNITY: WHAT IS IT?"

I glanced at my wrist to note the time, since there was no sun in the sky. My wrist had no watch on it, nor was there any telltale evidence of a watchband. In fact, the whole arm and body was of a beautiful, glowing, semi-transparent material without mar or scar. I gasped to realize that this was ME! (I would ask Jesus more about it later.) A strange sense of *timelessness* gripped me. It was simply awesome! I exclaimed: "Jesus, what happened to time, it seems to have vanished!" His disbelief at such a silly question in Paradise was evident in His Voice as He replied with loving restraint:[1]

"My child, The Book tells you clearly that all things seen or unseen, felt or unfelt, *are My creations*. Without Me nothing was made that was made. Originally there was nothing at all but the Everlasting God *in* Whom I am the Creator. That included what is known as 'time' in the universe of the firmament. Remember? I named Myself the 'Alpha and Omega,' the beginning and completion of all things. Remember? I took My beloved John to Heaven one day to foresee the fulfillments of My promises. He was so overwhelmed at seeing Me that I had to introduce Myself again as the '*Amen*, the *Faithful, True Witness*, and the *Beginning Creator* of the creations of God'! I had taken him ahead in 'earthly time' to the '*Day of the Lord*', the time of My victory over the works of Satan. We exist here in that timelessness, the eternity of God, the kind of Life that does not perish! It is our gift of Love, '*Eternal Life!*' "[2]

The simplicity of His explanation left me shaken. All that I could think was, "Of course!" Jesus had quietly restated that *Only* the Most High God could create anything. Neither an idol nor a man could do so! For *every* reason conceivable, *no one* less than God could make a universe without raw materials or Divine intelligence. History and common sense prove that: especially 'eternity' itself![3]

Expanding love and praise exploded within me as I sensed the immensity of the Person Who was talking to me so gently.

"You are Wonderful, Jesus. You do not think or act or promise in terms of 'time,' do You? Therefore your thoughts are unlimited. You can see all things as having happened already, even before they occur. That is how You can plan all events and creations to work together for the good of Your BODY and the glory of You, our Head! Even this paradise You made for me was prepared before I would arrive, wasn't it? You planned and planted all these fantastic trees, flowers, and grasses in my valley in advance of my coming here today, didn't You?"[4]

As if wreathed in smiles at my comprehension, He replied:

"Verily, My son! That is why *I* am *The Truth*, since no one but God *could* be. I am showing you now that what I said in My Book about death and Paradise, and even about My promise of you and Me being together as *one* in eternity, is The Truth. I and My Word are one also. Again I emphasize that I have written only Truth in My Book. I have begged My people 'to ask and seek and knock' as evidence of their *earnest* search for My everlasting love. So few ever do. Even My disciples failed to ask. I had to chide them by stating, 'Ye have not because ye ask not!'[5]

"I even made it very simple for them by promising if any two would agree upon a request, I would answer. I already had prepared the *right* answer in advance; by faith they were to accept it. That is how My Father, Our Spirit and I have arranged for all things to work together for those who love Us. I told them to abide *in* Me so that whatsoever they would seek would be *Our will* to give." Then Jesus paused as though disappointed in something.[6]

"Oh that My children *on earth* would believe Me! Oh that they would trust My Word, and would talk with Me! I gave them the *model* of how to pray; it is childlike because it is the expression of confidence. 'Our *Father*,!' He is the *Hallowed* God, the only God Who can help; the only God Who loves them and listens. I told them to request that 'His Kingdom come and His Will be *done on Earth*.' " That means now. Their mouths speak it but their hearts doubt it. How can He answer if they do not worship in spirit and in truth?[7]

"My gift is *eternal* life which has to *start on earth* where *they* need its cleansing power, and where *We* need our Good News of salvation *accepted*. Oh that My people would start their lives with Me there so they could *live abundantly* and not perish! Why do they want to wait and wait until it is too late?" His Voice seemed to drift off into a fog of sadness. I sensed that He was reliving a Gethsemane of agony where He had foreseen a world of people rejecting His Way to share their lives with Him. *It had made Him bleed!*[8]

He had explained about timelessness, so it now seemed a good "time" to inspect this paradise of mine a bit more closely. Nothing so grand could be imagined as a "walk" with Yeshua

Who could answer the swarms of questions forming in my new mind.

What a view!

END NOTES

1. I Cor. 15:38-44; Isa. 46:9-10 **2.** John 1:1-4; Heb. 11:3; Prov. 26:10; Col. 1:16-17; Ps. 90:2; II Peter 3:8; Gen. 1:1; Rev. 1:10; Rev. 3:14; Zeph. 1:14-17; John 3:16; II Cor. 4:18 **3.** Gen. 1:1; Jer. 10:10-13; Isa. 40:28; Heb 1:3 **4.** Isa. 9:6; Isa. 46:9-10; Isa. 44:24 **5.** Deut. 32:4; Ps. 117:2; John 14:6; Eph. 1:9-10; John 1:14-17; 2 Tim. 3:16; Matt. 7:7-8 **6.** James 4:3; Deut. 7:9; Rom. 8:28; John 15:7 **7.** Matt. 6:9-13; Jer. 17:7; Matt. 6:13; Matt. 6:6; John 4:23 **8.** Luke 2:10-11; John 10:10; John 14:5-6; Matt. 25:41; Luke 13:27

Question #5

"CREATED FOR PRAISE?"

What a place Jesus had prepared! I hung stock-still suspended in *weightlessness* a few feet above the flowered meadow. The ecstatic release from gravity in this new body was part of the permeating peace which surrounded me. Without time, I had no need to hurry.[1]

Music surrounded me. It came from all directions. Its harmonic beauty unlike earthly vocal or instrumental sounds was totally undistorted. It flowed unobtrusively like a glassy river, quietly worshipful, excitingly edifying, and totally comforting. It provided a reassuring type of comfort much like a protective blanket that whispered peace and love. I had never sensed anything like it. Perhaps "angelic" would describe it.[2]

This music was "sounding" within my head, not from an eardrum. Obviously it was not airborne. Most unusual to me was the absence of any "beat." Then I realized that without "time" this heavenly music could have *no beat* which is a measure of time! I was hearing harmonic perfection, undistorted by any interposed medium between me and its source, as heard mind-to-mind. I could wait no longer to ask:[3]

"Jesus, tell me about this wondrous music all about me. Who is the composer? How is it made? From whence does it come? It is gorgeous!"

I was not disappointed when He began His answer by again asking me: "*Didn't you read My Book?* Repeatedly it exhorts My children to *praise Me* with music from strings, trumpets, timbrels and voices. It is and was the prime communication of worship and praise and thanksgiving. Since I am the Creator, *I* am the Composer of heaven's music which you are hearing.[4]

"Music became the resulting harmony from all of our creations, both of matter and energy. All resonated in unison with Us. The elementary form was *of* and *from* and *in* Ourselves. I might explain it as a triad of sub-electronic energy particles with and around which We constructed everything in Our universe. The wave-forms We called Light; whereas the material-forms We called dust of the earth and water and air. Our of these, and into these, We created animals and birds and fishes and vegetable life to support them. Over these We created a mankind to supervise them as Our *appointed custodians* made in our special image to act *for Us* on earth!"[5]

Jesus hesitated as I tried to capture the immensity of His explanations.

"You must understand, My son, that original creation mirrored the composition and perfection of Person-God. All creation vibrated in unison with Us! There was total accord and harmony everywhere as the whole of creation was *resonating with* and *in* God! Each separate thing or being thus carried out an appointed task in Our scheme for the universe. A heaven-form of music resulted as even the stars sang in their appointed circuits. Here in Paradise you are hearing these melodious vibrations directly upon your new mind, undistorted. On earth you heard distorted sounds through the air waves. Throughout Heaven the music flows from My Throne, uninterrupted, undefiled, and peace-giving."[6]

Jesus paused again. "My Book tells of the time when Lucifer's *rebellion* in Heaven changed some things. He sought to usurp My Father's Throne, assume His position as The Most High God, and to rule the universe. For that blasphemy Lucifer was cast from Heaven to earth; in fact, *I* saw him fall as a bolt of lightning! In a tantrum of hate and rage over being deposed so fast he and his fallen angels disfigured Our perfect earth. It became void and uninhabitable. For punishment befitting this enemy of God, Lucifer was given a *new name, Satan,* since he was the self-appointed 'Adversary' of the Almighty. Anything that God had made, Satan would attempt to destroy from then on. As *Lucifer* he had been created the highest angel about the Throne, one of his assignments and talents being *the* chief musician in charge of *worship and music.* In his rebellious anger he set about destroying harmony on and in the earth from then on. That is why the earth where he operates now is out of harmony with God's other creations. In My Book we call this disharmony 'sin', because it defies God's Will that even the heavens declare the Glory of God and the firmament show His handiwork.[7]

"But be of good cheer, My son. The Father has permitted Me to overcome Satan's world's system of sin, and to destroy the *works* of Satan, and to *re-establish* righteousness in the hearts of My friends. Eventually in His chosen time He will restore *all* creation as it once was, *in Him!*"[8]

[It was clear enough that God's "heaven-music" was ever-present as a permeating *reminder* of the purity and power *in* its Creator. As God's methods of communication are headlined by music, even so is Satan's method of distorting its language to deceive through *his* "rock"! Jesus had clearly implied already that one of His final missions would be to *destroy* the very "works of the Devil" which include all music that fails to honor the Lord. Messiah promised to destroy any *disharmonies* which Satan uses to lure and deceive innocent children into the pits of hell!][9]

The music around me suddenly seemed louder. I rushed to a nearby tree and grasped its trunk to my ear: it was "singing." I lifted my right elbow to my head; it too emitted the same joyous, beatless melody. Excitedly I stopped to pick some flowers, and found them already in my hand. They too were "playing" the tune.[10]

END NOTES

1. Mark 9:2 **2.** II Sam. 6:5; Luke 19:38; John 14:27 **3.** Luke 24:39 **4.** Gen. 4:21; Ps. 104:33; Ps. 98:4-6; Ps. 100:1-2; Eph. 5:19-20; I Chr. 16:28 **5.** Col. 1:16-17; Gen. 1:1; John 1:1-2; Acts 17:24-27; Ps. 8:3-9; Gen. 1:24-31 **6.** Rom. 11:36; Job 35:10-11; Ps. 148:1-14; Job 38:7; Ps. 98:1 **7.** Ezek. 28:15,17; Isa. 14:12-15; Luke 10:18; Gen. 1:2; Ezek. 28:14-15; John 10:10; Ezek. 28:13b; Rev. 20:8; Ps. 19:1 **8.** I John 3:8; Rev. 20:10; Mark 1:24; Ps. 98:9; Heb. 2:14; John 16:33; I Cor. 15:28 **9.** Deut. 32:37; Mark 13:12; Ps. 150:3-6; I John 3:10; Matt. 18:6-7 10. Ps. 145:10-11

Question #6

"THE THOUGHT IS THE ACT?"

This bouquet in my hand made me gasp in wonderment for two reasons: it was so suddenly there in my hand without my having as yet picked it, and it was so exceedingly beautiful! I had merely thought about a bouquet, and there it was, ready for my inspection.

I was now gazing at stamens and pistils and calyces of transparent gold. Lengthwise through them I could see down into their stems. It was my first moment to see an example of heaven's liquid transparent gold? Such a thrill to share its beauty![1]

Then I noted the stems which filled my palm! Soft as velvet, and devoid of moisture, yet so alive! The pure-white petals, four to each flower, were identical, flawless, and picture-perfect. They seemed to be internally energized since all were emitting light of appropriate color.

I blurted out (mind-to-mind): "Jesus, I do not understand. I just decided to pick some flowers. They are already in my hand. I can see transparent golden centers, and their stems are water-less. I also sense that I am speaking with You through a new mind, with which I receive immediate answers!"

"My son," came the reply, "you are discovering how My mind works. Here in Paradise I have given you a portion of My MIND with which we communicate. You just discovered one of its properties: a thought in Heaven instantly becomes an act or a fact. DIDN'T YOU READ MY BOOK? In it I told My children that 'ye have the *Mind of Christ*' when you are *in* Me. On earth they too seldom use it. Here in Paradise it is the *Only* Mind. The earthly mind died with the carnal body; it was an enmity to Me! Flesh and blood can not inherit the Kingdom of God; only a righteous Mind is present in Heaven.[2]

"Here I speak mind-to-mind in My Heaven-language. My Word immediately performs My Will. It is Truth! To create, I think, and it is done. Of course, Satan has no power to interfere in this Heaven.[3]

"I hung the stars in space to tell of My protection and promises. When I wanted an earthly family to fellowship with Me, I *thought* of God's image, and it became a man who would live with life-flowing blood. I *thought* of animals, fish and birds: there they were, ready to eat the foods which I had carefully prepared for them that day. Even now, when I wish to bless My people, the power of My *thought* provides and transmits my blessings anywhere I send them.[4]

"My Book tells mankind that My thoughts are *not* as his are: his are vanity and evil and against Me. They come from the mind of unsaved man. There is *no power* in such thinking. To Me it is an abomination.[5]

"Because *I* am the Righteousness of God, My thoughts are precious and unlimited. Just as this Paradise is *far above* the earth, so are My thoughts are of peace and of goodwill toward men. My power sheds My love on them![6]

"When I created something new, I *did not need evolution! I AM* THE WORD. I am all that My Father needed to form, all that is seen from things not seen! Satan detests *Me* and every-thing I created, so he used a *theory* intended to *blaspheme* My power: a *lie and deception.* He still does. There is no truth in him anyway. He knows better: he was among the first and highest creations, but he fell through his overwhelming pride to an eventual eternity in Hell which was prepared for the punish-ment of him and his worshipers.[7]

"My son, your mind in Paradise works with the power of Mine. I give that very special privilege to all the children of God!"[8]

Jesus changed the subject: "You were amazed at the *gold* in the flowers. I enjoyed watching you discover that heavenly things are of a material unlike the dust of the earth. *Our gold* is pure and transparent and eternal. My Light shines through it. I created it that way as a gift to *My* Father! It bespeaks His per-fection."[9]

Jesus hastened to explain more. "You were wondering about those 'dry' stems. My Book would have told you that Heaven has none of *earth's* matter since it was cursed because of sin. Satan lied and *did* deceive Eve, and then Adam, into sinning against their Creator-God. In Heaven, which includes Paradise, there are no gases such as hydrogen and oxygen from which *I made water* on earth. On earth it is essential to maintain life. It is a substitute for what we have *here*, LIVING WATER! Earthly water has become *polluted*. Living Water is always *pure*. It flows from My Throne. One drop can last for eternity. Remem-ber? I told the woman at the well that she should ask of Me a drop of that Living Water. She was so excited that she sent a crowd of her friends running to meet Me![10]

"Earth's water has been so dirtied by man that I will some-day have to *destroy* all of it, and remake the old earth with a new one without even a sea![11]

"My son, you know that everything in all of Heaven is sustained by My LIVING WATER. Your flowers are one example which I let you discover so that you would ask Me for an answer. Your flowers are watered from My Throne through My Spirit. You noted the absence of any fallen leaves. My *Living Water* prevents leaves from dying; it does not evaporate! All forms of life here are maintained by My Light and My Living Water. Both are pure and eternal. I told you in My Book about these leaves: they are for the *healing* of the Nations! And I told you that I would be the *Light of Heaven*, and no curse can exist in My Light![12]

"At the time of Creation We ordered each life form to multiply 'after its own kind,' including *new mankind*. We made them male and female so that their union in procreation would *mirror the bond* of loving *unity* which exists between the Father in Heaven and His family on earth. That is My Father's *greatest* love! He even had Me shed My blood and die in order to re-establish *that* relationship as an *eternal* gift![13]

"My son, the time is coming when *Satan* will be bound in a bottomless pit for a thousand years awaiting his banishment into eternal punishment in a lake of fire! His reign of terror on the earth will have ended. No longer will he be allowed to corrupt the minds and families of man. His worldwide rule over the nations will have been suddenly ended. I will rule instead! As I told you in My Book, with Satan gone I will create a new Heaven and Earth and a new city Jerusalem. My peace and grace will abound (instead of every kind of sin and hate as have existed on earth since Babylon because man chose to worship the Devil). The whole universe will then be set free to worship the Righteous God."[14]

****

Five years after this conversation with me, Jesus re-appeared to me in Lazarus' Tomb with an amazing command: "Go tell them what I explained to you in Paradise when I let you die for a while!" I have been attempting to speak and write words ever since of that fantastic moment, but no human language is at all adequate. However, I pray that some words here have been meaningful to someone. Jesus promised that He would see to that! (This is His story too.)[15]

****

Suddenly, as the Risen Lord paused in His explanation of future glories in a righteous universe, I realized that the new body I had in this Paradise had not once signalled its presence to my mind. I had been oblivious of its existence while Yeshua was talking. And yet it was "me," and vitally alive. This raised another question.

END NOTES

1. Matt. 6:28-29; Rev. 21:18; Rev. 3:18; I Pet. 1:7 **2.** John 10:28; Heb. 11:3; I Cor. 2:16: Phil. 2:13; Rom. 8:7; I Cor. 3:19-20 **3.** Heb. 1:3; John 14:30 **4.** Gen. 1:15; Isa. 55:11 **5.** Isa. 55:8; Ps. 94:11; Ps. 56:5; Mark 7:21-23; Prov. 15:26 **6.** Isa. 55:8-9; Ps. 139:17-18; Isa. 55:9; Jer. 29:10-11; I John 4:19 **7.** Gen. 2:1-2,19; Mal. 2:10; John 1:3; I Cor. 1:23-24; Matt. 28:18; John 8:44; Rev. 20:7,10; Rev. 21:8 **8.** Jer. 10:12; John 1:12 **9.** Rev. 21:21; Rev. 3:18 **10.** Gen. 3:4-5, 17-19; John 4:13; John 7:37-39; Isa. 44:3; John 4:13-14 **11.** Rev. 8:11; Isa. 65:17; Rev. 21:1 **12.** Rev. 21:6; Rev. 22:1,17; Ps. 148:4-6; Rev. 22:2; John 12:35-36; Rev. 22:5 **13.** Gen. 1:24; Gen. 2:27; Gen. 4:1; John 3:16; Rom 6:23; John 12:49-50; Heb. 9:14 **14.** Rev.

20:1-2,10; Isa. 14:15; Rev. 18:1-5; Rev. 21:1; Mic. 4:1; Isa. 66:23; Rev. 19:16; Rev. 22:3-7 15. Isa. 55:11; Num. 23:19; Jer. 1:6-8; Ps. 19:14

Question #7
"A CELESTIAL BODY?"

These events in Paradise had occurred with such lightning-like speed that I had not inspected my totally comfortable new body. It was unbelievable, as was everything else up there![1]

I was recognizable as "me." My shape, size, and appearance would indicate that I had been changed suddenly into an un-marred, unscarred, weightless "me." This was Dick Eby in some new form! My amazement grew with each part that I inspected. Never had I seen anything like it. Was I "in" a new body, or was I "the" new body? I could not tell. (To this day I do not know; neither did St. Paul who sagely described his similar experiences as "unutterable," not knowing whether he was "in or out of the body." He said that it was "celestial.")[2]

Its material fascinated me. Obviously of a substance *peculiar* to Heaven, it was *modestly glowing*, transparent to the direct gaze, yet semi-solid at times. Looking down at my feet, I was shocked to see myself not touching the solid ground, although I had felt a thud when I had suddenly arrived there. I *hung gracefully* above the lush grasses of this meadow. I noted stemmed flowers with glowing white petals standing quietly within my legs up to the kneecaps. I saw no muscles nor nerves, no vessels nor bones, just that homogeneous glass-like "*spirit-matter*"! Obviously these flowers ignored my presence, just as

I did not feel theirs. Reflexly I feared lest I had damaged these heavenly flowers by landing upon them; I would lift my right leg off them. Before finishing my thought, the leg was raised, and the flowers remained motionless and perfect. I gasped. My *thought* had lifted the leg as it was being simultaneously "processed." I heard myself think: "That's exciting; I will lower my leg back over the flowers and see what happens." Nothing was felt; not a petal moved within my leg. It was amazing.[3]

A "Physical Exam of a Spirit-Body"

The ecstasy of being "free indeed" in a new place and a new body made me feel like a spirited calf loosed from a stall. I decided to run around my paradise and learn more about it and me. At the thought, I was running without touching the ground. Although my legs were in motion, my speed changed with my thoughts. I came to a tree and passed throughout it without feeling anything. I kicked my feet through the grasses, bushes, and beds of flowers; nothing was disturbed. They simply passed through my legs with no resistance. I was rapidly learning that a "spirit body" and this heavenly vegetation are not of any earthly substance.[4]

I stopped running to inspect *my own body* more closely. It was homogeneous. As I gazed through it I was surprised to see *no organs*. It apparently functioned without members of differing secretions and excretions! It was immediately logical to me that in Heaven there is no need for a body to ingest, digest, transform, reform, nor to "process" foods or waste! In Heaven there is no polluted water nor air nor chemical to attack the spirit body. There is not even any unclean thought to be rejected![5]

This *new spirit body* had no restrictions imposed by an outer or inner environment of solids, gases, or waste. What excitement! I was enjoying dashing effortlessly around the huge valley floor of flowering meadows, and up the mountainsides to the stately, symmetrical "cedars of Lebanon" (as my mind was silently naming them).[6]

I tried to cast my shadow across the underlying fields as I swooped along. Everything was so brightly lit. It seemed abnormal not to see shadows so I flailed my arms: nothing. The Light of Heaven was coming from no one source, but was emitted everywhere in appropriate colors. Each a bit of vegetation seemed to contain a light source of its own. So did I.[7]

Reflexly I raised my arms in thanks and adoration for my Lord's love in showing me Heaven's wonders which were mysteries to me. As I bowed my head, I noted a glowing *pure-white gown* which somehow I had not seen when I looked through it in search of organs! I was awed by its total weightlessness and silky softness. My raised arms had parted its overlapping folds for the moment, revealing me as a neuter! This came as a shock, although I had not felt surprise at the absence of defects or scars. This alteration was so unexpected![8]

"Lord Jesus, why am I now a *neuter*? I was a man."

"Yes, Dick, you were always a man, a child of God who returned Our love by telling others of the Good News about Me. Remember? You read in My Book the very first order I gave to Adam and Eve: '*Be fruitful and multiply!*' I told them to replenish the Earth, *not* Heaven. Again I told the Sadducees (who did not believe in a Resurrection) that they 'knew not the Scriptures' when they speculated about wives in Heaven. I explained that after resurrection all would be like angels who do not marry nor raise families. Everything in Heaven is created or re-created into perfection! It is all in *My* Book. None other is Truth![9]

"In fact, *everything* that My children *need to know* about how God thinks and works and judges and rewards, either before or after the Cross, *is already in My Book*. That is why I *commanded* mankind to 'engrave My Words upon their hearts,' and to pass them along from generation to generation. I wanted everyone to hear and know just Who I AM, the Messiah, their one hope of Salvation, their Most High God."[10]

I checked my body again: truly celestial! Its senses were too keen to describe. (Weightless, painless, instantly responsive. Comfortable and totally peaceful. Unaware of any disharmony elsewhere. Thinking with the mind of Christ. Sensing that I was *IN* Him somehow). He had said so clearly, "I and the Father are One." He had prayed so fervently "that they all may be one, as Thou, Father, art in Me, and I in Thee; that they may be also *one in Us!*," the Father declared it done![11]

The very contemplation of experiencing this fulfillment of being in Paradise with the risen Jesus was unutterable. To know that I, in this *spirit body*, was actually in some glorious sense *IN* Him for eternity staggered even the imagination of my *new* mind. It was so obvious that Dick Eby had not of himself merited any such glory.

****

(I was to realize later when I reviewed *His Book* that He had truly put in it *His* explanation of why a *Believer* can hope for an after-earth eternal life: There it was all the time:

There is therefore now no condemnation to them which are *in* Christ Jesus, who walk not after the flesh but after the Spirit!

He *was* Christ: I was *IN* Him. That made us ONE, and *this* was Paradise, just as Jesus foresaw would be ours someday if we would pray to His Father: "Thy Will be done on *Earth* as in Heaven!" What a glorious plan He has for His children!)[12]

****

Jesus Explained This Abundant Joy

Events in Paradise were occurring unbelievably fast. Thoughts and actions there seemingly vie with each other to be completed instantly. The environment of Heaven with its time-lessness, weightlessness, and lack of all earthly confusion and stress results in a type of "joy" unattainable in this world system. I simply stood (floated) quietly, peacefully, entranced in an experience which only a Living, Loving God could have arranged for His followers![13]

Jesus all this time seemed to be a component of myself, of my spirit body and of my mind. He must have been amused at my near-delirious joy while inspecting the place He had prepared for my pleasure.

"My son, you seem to be enjoying the freedoms of Heaven! You looked surprised especially over your spirit body which is so different from your *former* one. That is one reason that I had allowed it to die so that I could reveal to you another truth which My Book contains. You now know that My Book is true when I promise *complete* healing as part of salvaging My sheep from sin. I had to prepare an *incorruptible body* to replace the fleshly one that had been cursed ever since Adam disobeyed me in the Garden.[14]

"In order not to break My own verdict, I had to sentence Adam's seed to 'surely die' because he followed Satan's advice. I had to leave the *seeds of death in* his flesh. My Book says that I can and will *mend* man's body when it will result in glory to My Father; but I do not give '*Divine*' health to the carnal body: only to the spirit or resurrection form. Death of the *dust-body* (not the human spirit) is still a Divine Decree. Only through rebirth of the spirit in a *new creation* (which will *transform* man completely) can an incorruptible body be attained, fit for eternal existence *in* and *with* Me! I made that fact so clear by dying and arising in My *new* body! *I was the Example.* I told My disciples that they would follow Me in *that newness* of life. A few understood finally, after seeing Me ascend to Heaven![15]

"My Father empowered Me to act as 'a Quickening Spirit' in order to raise the dead, in body and spirit. Remember? I told that secret to Mary and Martha: '*I* am the resurrection *and* the life!' Then I demonstrated how My Father had given power to Me (for *His* purpose) when needed. They watched, and they believed! *YOU* are here now because I passed you from death unto life!"[16]

END NOTES

1. I Cor. 15:40-50 **2.** James 2:26; II Cor. 12:2-3; I Cor. 15:40 **3.** I Cor. 15:50; I Cor. 15:39-40 **4.** Mal. 4:2; Luke 24:30-31; I Cor. 15:35 **5.** Luke 24:41-43; I Cor. 15:44 **6.** Mark 16:14; Mark 9:4; 16:12,14; John 21:14 **7.** Isa. 60:1,19-20; I Pet. 2:9-10; Matt. 5:16; I John 1:5-7; Eph. 5:8-11; II Cor. 6:14; Rev. 21:23-25 **8.** Rev. 3:5; Matt. 17:2; Matt. 28:3 **9.** Gen. 1:28; Isa. 45:18; Matt. 22:29-30; Gal. 6:15; Jer. 32:17; Heb. 1:10 **10.** II Tim. 2:15; II Tim. 3:16-17; Deut. 6:5-7; Ps. 78:4-6; II Tim. 3:15 **11.** John 14:20; John 17:20-23; Eph. 1:10,13 **12.** Rom. 15:4; Rom. 8:1; Matt. 6:10 **13.** Heb. 4:12; Isa. 11:3: Eph. 5:1-2 **14.** II Cor. 3:17-18; John 8:36; II Cor. 5:8; Gen. 3:3 **15.** Rom. 7:5-6; II Cor. 5:17; Eph. 4:23-24; Rom. 6:3-10 **16.** I Cor. 15:45-47; John 11:25-26; John 12:45; John 5:24-25

Question #8

"PERFUME? MARRIAGE?"

Already this Paradise of marvels had supplied enough wonders! Any earthly dreams about "heavenly mansions" had been corrected and surpassed. No memories of earth remained with me except the ones which Jesus was obviously implanting in my new mind in order to understand what He had to tell me. His mind-to-mind conversation from within me was unbelievably precise as to meaning, and as fast as lightning. What a Teacher![1]

I just stood still, surveying the peace-filled valley, quiet except for the background music that flowed through and around everything. The brilliant light of Heaven filled the "sky" without hurting the eyes of my "spirit body." No sense of fatigue or need for sleep existed in this body. There was no "time", no "daylight" savings! No hurry, hurry.

Then I noticed something amazingly delightful: I was bathed in a delicate perfume, totally "heavenly!" I had been smelling it all along, but was too excited to stop and sniff its absolute loveliness. It seemed to permeate the landscape and me. I imagined that whatever it was, it was certainly fit *only* for a King![2]

"Jesus," I exclaimed, "What is this perfume? Do angels use it? Where does it come from?"

Silence. I repeated the query. Still no answer. Perhaps the Lord would answer later? (He did! But not in Heaven).

My Heavenly Valley

Hearing no answer, I turned my gaze toward the far end of my valley. Again I gasped at its grandeur. Tall rolling hills stretched into the distant sky, skirted at their feet with green meadows trimmed in white and gold flowers. My mind was reminding me of Jesus's comment about "lilies of the field" whose adornment surpassed the elegance of Solomon.[3]

I was peacefully examining a cluster of intriguingly lovely lilies (kind unknown to me) when an unexpected strangeness suddenly seemed to crush me. (I had been enjoying my paradise all this time; the reality of being "at Home" had become a normal situation which can best be described as an immersion into total peace, unending and perfect!) It was as though a subtle "change in plans" had now occurred: my perfect peace seemed to "crack." An unexplained restlessness crept into me, and a memory formed in my mind for the first time: Where is Maybelle, my loving, lovely wife on earth? We were so close that she must have died too. She must be up here in her very own paradise. I must find her and take her a bouquet of these lovely flowers. She would so enjoy them. Where do I find her? I feel so lonesome.[4]

I looked away from the flowers at my feet, just as a narrow path suddenly parted the lush grass, as if a rushing blade had mowed a strip from my feet to the far end of the valley. Just as suddenly we *both* were running along (but just above) this pathway. I shouted to Jesus:[5]

"What is happening? Where am I headed? Why do I suddenly remember my Maybelle? I must find her!"

"My son, fear not! You remembered about her because I put it upon your mind that she was part of you. I wanted you to understand why My Father and I made marriage something very special. I wrote in My Book a warning: 'Let no man put asunder what God has united!' We were planning the earthly family to be as close-knit as is our Heavenly family, *like a mirror-image!*"[6]

Just then I noted that our speed along the path was rapidly accelerating, and that a curve to the right was visible far ahead where the path disappeared into a pass.

"You are feeling 'incomplete' all at once because your other half is 'missing.' We made the two of you one! I want you to experience something *right now* in Paradise with Me which you could not sense elsewhere! I am letting you feel 'intense hurt,' *the hurt of lonesomeness*, such as *I* have felt from being separated from *My* earthly people for so long! Remember? I told Adam that it is not good to be alone as a man! Since he was made in *Our* image, the same applies to God. We choose a family once: We espoused Israel and Judah as the Wife of Jehovah. She and We would walk and work together to bring down the idol worship of Satan's nations who rejected their Creator.[7]

"But *Our wife Israel* chased after other gods, and played the whore and 'slept' with Satan. Jehovah (Who includes Me) had to obey His own Laws, so We gave her a bill of divorcement. We had to chasten her until she would repent: otherwise We would be breaking Our own rules! Since then she has not yet repented, and is still wandering like *lost sheep*.[8]

"I am *lonesome* for My people to come Home to Me. I even came to Earth to win them back, but they said 'Away with Him! Crucify Him!' I left them a promise that *I still love them*. After all I even died for them. I promised that I would restore My divorcee and would wash her filthy rags of whoredom white as snow. I would make *her* my new Bride adorned in a pure white wedding gown with jewels. As a wedding present *I would re-establish her Nation* on earth to be a *blessing* once again (instead of the stumbling *stone*). I must be her King on David's Throne! And soon![9]

"The Father and I have *felt so neglected* all these centuries without the love we sought to enjoy with our Family. Can you now imagine how We hurt as I await My Body and *My Father* waits to remarry a *penitent wife* as Our new bride? I am letting *you* feel that sense of separation!"[10]

Only the rush of our speed could have turned my attention away from Jesus' profound statements. The bend in the path was approaching in the distance, so Jesus hastened to finish His lesson in marriage: "My son, the most important earthly gift that We can give to our children is a mate! Their marriage is meant to reflect the *inseparable bond* of love which unites Us with Our sheep in Our fold! We become *ONE* with them, just as we intend marriage to make one out of two on earth! That is what happens when a man and his mate let *Us* put them together. I said so in My Book which is My Love-Letter to Our Family on earth![11]

"Oh that My people would turn back now to God! My Father is unwilling that any should perish, but *very few listen to Us*. Their eyes and ears are sealed over by sins which they enjoy. It simply makes Our search for the lost ones all the more intense! I have prepared and promised them *unsearchable riches* in Our presence; in fact everything that I have received from the Father I have willed over to them, jointly! I want *My Body* of believers completed *very soon*, so that the Bride can be united in *Us* at the Marriage Table! *I* am their Lamb. If only My people would call on Me, I could answer them *now*! Do you sense my loneliness? *I* am ready; why must *they* tarry?"[12]

My Exit From Paradise

I was about to respond when the pathway above which was speeding took a sharp right turn into a narrow valley. As I swooped between its foothills I gasped at a familiar voice that echoed from somewhere far ahead: "*Dick, where are you? Follow my voice. I need you!*" Like a bolt of lightning-speed I was suddenly being shot forward. Her voice became louder and louder. I was being sucked forward as if by a huge vacuum and then, into total blackness and blankness! No Voice, no nothing. I had been sent out of Paradise. Why?

I would learn later. Plans *had* been changed! Maybelle had been frantically praying for a miracle: and Jesus had answered![13]

The Answer

In God's planning, my time in Paradise had fulfilled what He wanted to accomplish for me *there*. He had left Maybelle *on earth* to accomplish for her another purpose!

It would take many months for us to be shown how the horror of her day of widowhood (with its blood, sirens, and questionings, and waitings, and shocking hopeless reports) could possibly be "to the Glory of God"! The numbing sudden loss of her loved one had initially erased from her mind the details which require immediate answers at such a time of accident. So she prayed, "Help me, Jesus! I don't know what to do!" And then it happened.[14]

Maybelle's Recollection:

As the ambulance unloaded the muddy, blood-covered corpse she sensed an *umbrella of peace* settling over her. As she told me later, her strength and mind seemed to mount up "like an eagle" just as her hand-worn Bible had promised. All during the day-long hours of discouraging reports from confused doctors, she found herself being used to minister to bereaved families who felt hopeless. She began to wonder: "Did my Dick have to die just to get me here to tell others about a Living Lord? So few know about Him as a *Comforter!*"[15]

Later that night she was instructed to check in at an adjoining motel to try to get some sleep and to await a phone call regarding disposition of the corpse once the undiagnosed blips on the oscilloscope ceased. "Due to regulations, the bloodless body cannot be sent to the funeral parlor 'blipping': apparently there is some electrical interference affecting the equipment tonight. You will be called as soon as the situation is corrected. The coroner cannot do the autopsy till the tracings are straight," she was told.

A very new day (for both of us) was about to dawn.

END NOTES

1. I Cor. 2:9; Matt. 5:17-18 **2.** Gen. 8:21; II Cor. 2:15; Rev. 8:3 **3.** Matt. 6:28-29 **4.** Ps. 23:6; Eph. 2:19 **5.** Prov. 12:28; Ps. 16:11 **6.** Eph. 5:23-24; Matt. 19:4-6; Eph. 3:15 **7.** Gen. 2:18; Jer. 2:7-20; Jer. 3:8-10; Exod. 20:3-5 **8.** Ezek. 16:36-38; Jer. 2:32,34; Jer. 3:8-10; Isa. 53:6; Luke 11:49-50; Jer. 50:6 **9.** Ps. 77:7-9; Ps. 103:8-12; Isa. 44:21,23; Heb. 8:8-12;

Jer. 31:31-32; Rev. 7:14; Hos. 2:16-20; Rev. 19:7; Rev. 21:4-6; Matt. 27:37; Isa. 35:10; Isa. 65:18-19; Isa. 64:4 **10.** Isa. 25:9 **11.** Deut. 7:6-8; Gen. 2:24; Matt. 19:3-6; Mal. 2:14-16 **12.** Isa. 55:7; Ps. 7:11-12; Ezek. 33:11; 12:2; Isa. 11:11-12; Eph. 3:8; Rom. 8:32; Rev. 19:7-9; Zeph. 3:17 **13.** Phil. 4:6-7; Ps. 55:22 **14.** Ps. 120:1; Ps. 121:2-3,8; Rev. 4:11; Heb. 13:5; Heb. 4:16; Eph. 3:12 **15.** Isa. 53:4; Isa. 40:13; Ps. 27:13; Acts 23:6; Rom. 15:13; I Thess. 4:13; II Thess. 2:16-17

PART TWO

RETURN TO EARTH WITH JESUS AND HIS WORD

Question #9
"YOU MUST BE KIDDING?"

Out of the jet-black darkness and total silence that followed Maybelle's summons, the next thing that I can remember was a *sense* of dropping for miles downward through broken, black fog banks into a blinding light. Amazingly, it was the same kind of *light* that filled Paradise! My spirit-self was suddenly on Earth.[1]

At that moment I was again given the *mind of Christ* that He had given me in Glory. With it, I was surveying a hospital room with spirit eyes. I saw a corpse whose gray stiff body lay bloodless with oscilloscope leads stuck in it. (As in Paradise, these *new eyes* could see in all directions). The battered face was mine! In that instant a thought crossed "my" mind: "So this is how you got to Heaven. An accident damaged your head, and it bled you out!"[2]

I noted through the window that it was now night time. A tiny baseboard lamp was shining upon a sleepy nurse with a pad and pencil. This place was anything but Heaven! A hospital!

Suddenly through a *heavenly light* that filled the room there appeared a more brilliant object emerging through the plaster. My eyes locked upon a spot just below the ceiling at the far end of the room. Inch by inch, brighter and brighter, a *cloud entered silently* and floated along the ceiling. It was about two to three feet long and half as thick. It was gold and white all at the same time. Obviously I was seeing it with Spirit-Body eyes! For a moment it hung motionless above me, then settled gracefully just above my right thigh. Its beauty was exquisite. I gasped, knowing suddenly that this was *Jesus' Shekinah Glory Cloud*, His Divine Covering when He visited Earthly children with special messages; it *revealed* His Glory and *protected* His priests! It had enshrouded Him when He ascended above the awe-struck disciples long ago!)[3]

Out of the Cloud came The Voice—so familiar now! *None other* is like it! Regal, majestic, captivating, authoritative, dynamic, yet meek and loving:

"My son, MY PEACE I GIVE UNTO YOU. WITH YOUR HANDS YOU WILL HEAL!"[4]

I was stunned. No stranger announcement could He have given to a corpse! It seemed only a moment ago when He had given me Heavenly peace as we talked in Paradise. There I was *totally alive*. How could I be at peace as a dead man? And certainly *I* could not heal anything now! Without hesitation a voice came *from* my mouth: "YOU MUST BE KIDDING!"[5]

The Cloud neither moved nor winced. I felt ashamed and astounded at being so rude to My guest, the Lord of Lords. What would He do now? I awaited a rebuff, at least a rebuke. Instead, from the Cloud came the same assurance again: "MY PEACE I GIVE UNTO YOU. WITH YOUR HANDS YOU WILL HEAL!"[6]

As though suddenly sensing an emergency *elsewhere*, Jesus concluded in lightning-like speed: "By this I mean that I will restore your body to life and your skills for practice. But more than that, I will be answering your many prayers that I use your hands for healing those diseases which *I* alone can handle. I have been doing this for you all of the time that you were practicing, but I did not tell you each time. Now I will let you see and enjoy the signs and wonders of healing as you lay on hands in My Name. All I want in return is *your* praise and *theirs*. Therein I can bestow My Peace as you work with ME!"[7]

The Agony of The Lamb!

Just as a voice from me said "Thank You, Jesus," something happened that to this day makes me shudder in agony. It doubtless lasted hardly a second, but that was too long. My dead body was being wracked with total pain transcending any that a living body could have felt!

I would have either screamed or convulsed or gone insane from any such agony in a breathing body. As a corpse I lay there as if in Hell, screaming in the mind that had been put in it for this moment while the Cloud was present:[8]

"Please, Jesus, *HELP*! Do something. I can't take it! Every cell in my body is separately being tortured. I can feel each different kind of cell hurting in its special way. Don't leave me now! Don't forsake me like this. Please HELP!" I was shouting to Him mind-to-mind.[9]

I did not have to wait. As in Paradise His answer overlaid my cry. "Fear not, My son. I never leave you nor forsake you. My Book told you that! I want you to understand more about Me *before* I put life back into your body. I would not torture your body afterwards! Do you remember that before the foundation of the world God designated a part of Himself as The *LAMB*? That was My very first Name, a Name above all others. The LAMB of God was to bear all the sins and diseases of *men*. God asked Me if I was willing to die and bleed as a Sacrifice acceptable in place of them. I said, 'Thy Will be done!' "[10]

"We went through a rehearsal. Right then I was slain *in Jehovah's eyes* so that no legal loophole could ever be conceived in Lucifer's mind once he became Our rebellious adversary, Satan! He could never claim that I had died too late to save souls of My people already created. Jehovah required that 'I suffer' at that moment in Heaven in anticipation of what He would later require when I would come as 'Son' and be hanged on a bloody cross. God wanted me to know also the agony of having *Him* forsake Me for that moment when I would appear to Him as the 'Sin of The World' hanging there! I have known *all* the sins and pains of My created children; I have felt them *separately* and *keenly*. I have agonized for them![11]

"Now you may use your suffering as a witness of *My martyrdom* when you describe how I died to save souls from Satan's Hell! It is totally agonizing when My Father and I must watch our people rejecting My gift of Life by selecting Satan's *death* sentence. You see, My son, I was the *Righteous Sacrifice* from the very beginning. Therefore no sin or sorrow is too great for Me to cleanse or comfort. I had to die only once to be the Redeemer of *all* mankind. I paid the price. I shouted to My Father from the Cross, 'It is finished.' I had *bought back* from Satan any claim that he could make about the world or its people. I silenced him in Heaven's court *that* day!"[12]

(My agony abruptly ended as did Jesus' *horror* story as the Amazing Lamb. Like a huge vacuum I felt the terrible pains being sucked from my "middle" out through the arms and legs, leaving the body painless.)

"I was not 'kidding' when I told you just now that you would be restored to life! I used that word intentionally because you can use it effectively when you tell about *this day* with Me. Nor was I 'kidding' when I agreed to being the LAMB slain to save lost sheep, no matter what *price*! I did *not 'kid'* you when

I promised to prepare a place for us to live together *after I died* and arose. You have been there. I do *not 'kid' anyone* about the truths in My Book. I AM Truth. I AM Life. I AM Resurrection Power; I will show you *today*. I am not kidding! I will be back to heal you!"[13]

Instantly the Cloud lifted slowly from my thigh, floated to the far end of the room, and disappeared through the plastered wall. As it left the room the light vanished: all was black, and I was blank again. Without Jesus present, I had no life nor mind in the stilled body.[14]

****

Several days later I would learn about other happenings as that night wore on. According to reports, the oscilloscopes' "static-blips" had stopped at around 6 A.M.! Maybelle's motel phone had awakened her, requesting that she return to the hospital to sign out the body to a funeral home.

She had rushed to the bedside where she saw my body for the first time since the accident the morning before. She noted that the thick head-bandage covering the much-sutured scalp was lying beside the still, battered head. Bending closer she saw that the 196 stitches (which the emergency doctor had placed to approximate the strips of scalp before the anticipated funeral) were holding *healed* tissue. Reassured that her Lord was answering yesterday's frantic prayers *without* her help, she strode to the cafeteria for a quiet breakfast, rather than sign the discharge forms! She felt at peace.[15]

****

That morning was to be one to remember.

END NOTES

1. Rev. 21:23; Rev. 22:5; Ps. 36:9; Mal. 4:2 **2.** I Cor. 2:16; Prov. 15:3; Prov. 23:26 **3.** Exod. 16:10; Exod. 14:20; Exod. 13:21-22; Exod. 24:16; I Kings 8:10; Luke 21:27; Isa. 60:19-20; Acts 1:9 **4.** Exod. 24:16b; Isa. 45:15,18 **5.** Mark 16:18b; John 14:27; Acts 28:8; John 5:21 **6.** Titus 1:2; Acts 4:30 **7.** Deut. 5:22; Mark 16:18; John 14:12; I John 4:4 **8.** Matt. 13:40-43; Ps. 88:1,16 **9.** Ps. 28:1; Ps. 22:14: Ps. 6:2-3 **10.** Heb. 13:5; Rev. 13:8; Gen. 22:8; John 1:29,36; Heb. 10:12 **11.** Rev. 5:6,12; I Pet. 1:19; Rev. 7:14; Heb. 9:26,28; Isa. 53:6,10,19; I Pet. 2:22,24 **12.** Rom. 5:8; John 3:36; Eph. 2:8-9; I Pet. 2:21-25; I Pet. 3:18; John 19:30 **13.** Acts 20:28; Heb. 13:20; II Cor. 12:3-4; Col. 1:5; Gal. 2:5,16; John 14:6 **14.** Eccles. 9:10; Ps. 88:5-6 **15.** Isa. 53:5; Matt. 4:24

Question #10

"A TIME FOR HEALING?"

Maybelle's morning hospital visit was obviously unnoticed by me, but not by Jesus. He was fulfilling two promises which He had joyfully made a long time before this particular morning. For Maybelle He was bringing His gift of perfect *peace*. For me He was coming with *Healing* in His wings! He had said, "I will be back today."[1]

Apparently Maybelle had just left the room when I was suddenly given His Mind again. The jet-blackness and mental blankness were erased as by a Divine Hand. Immediately The Voice was speaking. My Healer was present yet unseen:[2]

"I am here, My son, to complete My promise that you will live. I WILL MEND YOUR BODY AND BRAIN SO THAT YOUR HEALING WILL RESTORE YOU TO WORK FOR ME."[3]

This time there was no Cloud nor bright light. He was working in the dark as I lay inert with the electric leads attached to head and heart. He first gave me enough of *His* Mind so that we could converse as before. I was *so* excited. This "Presence" seemed to rush around *in* my body. We kept up a constant discussion as to where to start, how to repair crushed or torn nerve trunks, and when to connect vessels to inert organs! I made many suggestions which He wisely ignored! We were both ecstatic as sensations returned and feeble motions started in my extremities. The awesome wonder of it all overwhelmed me, and delighted Him.[4]

Gently, carefully, deftly my Healer handled the tissues with loving care. Repeatedly He paused to ask if I understood what He was doing. Then He would ask what I thought should be done next! Naturally, He had better ideas. Cells and organs were responding to *His Presence*. Suddenly my own brain took over with its sluggish thoughts, registering the numerous pains from head to heels. Hands quivered, eyelids raised slowly, and tremors developed in hands and legs. The faint light of dawn through the window revealed that my eyes could see only waterfalls over shadowy outlines of objects in the room. The ears were ringing like thousands of bells. But *I WAS ALIVE! Jesus had come and touched me!!* I would see my Maybelle again! (I faintly remembered her calling for me "long" ago. Now I was here, back on earth. Surely she would find me soon.) I whispered weakly: "Perhaps now would be a good time, while I rest a bit, to ask Jesus again about that Heavenly perfume."[5]

Silently I prayed: " Thank you, Jesus, for restoring my life." (I was now thinking in English). "But please do not leave without telling me about that *Heavenly perfume*. I want to be thinking about it while I am resting. I want to tell Maybelle too." I realized my spoken words would be too blurred to be understood. My lips and tongue were punctured and numb, with strings of flesh caught in my teeth. My jaw wouldn't move right. The mouth and throat were still 'dead.'[6]

Scarcely had I prayed when I heard the answer on my mind. This time in English The Voice was calm, clear, and very slow. I could imagine that He was looking me over as He spoke, as though appraising the body's functions after my efforts to use it. It seemed to me that He was assessing what might still be needed to put it in running order for whatever future purposes He had in mind! His reply was brief:

"SEARCH THE SCRIPTURES; IN THEM YOU WILL FIND THE TRUTH."[7]

The brevity surprised me. I tried to recall any Bible references that pertained to perfume. I discovered that my brain contained no verses at all! I was in panic to know why:

"Please don't leave yet, Jesus! Why did You not replace any Bible verses in my memory where I had stored many before I died? I feel lost without them. They comforted me. What happened?"[8]

There was a pause as though He had to come back to answer me:

"You did not yet have them memorized correctly *with* understanding. I want you to start over and do it right this time!"[9]

Another pause, and the Presence was gone. He had left me to search and study on my own, as the body and mind which He had *touched* would complete its needed healing. Due to the cellular laws which He had established at Creation *He* knew that I would get well. Now it was time for *me* to get going on my own![10]

****

I glanced around the empty room though my eyes were still full of dancing lights as if seeing through a waterfall. Daylight was filling the room. And I suddenly needed a rest room!

Gingerly I tested my legs: yes, the toes moved slowly. And I could move my hips. Then I noticed the electric leads attached to my chest and arms and head. My neck was lying to one side, apparently broken, but was turned toward a bedside stand on which was a bottle of cottonballs. Painfully I reached for one, pulled out the nearest needle, and stuck it in the cotton. One by one I removed all the leads and tried to sit up. The room spun at first then settled down! "Praise God, I'll make it," said a little voice inside! I slid to the edge of the high bed, and swung my stiff feet toward the floor.[11]

Just then the door burst open, and there stood Maybelle, aghast at what she saw! Without time to think, she shouted, "Dick, what are you doing? Lie down or you will fall and kill yourself again!" With a leap she grabbed her "swaying husband" and pushed me back down to the pillow. The next hour was another miracle.

****

It was "60 minutes" that I shall not forget. (Maybelle who has since gone to be with Jesus in Paradise may be even now sitting at His feet as they share memories of that unique morning of unbelievable events including our laughter together!)

"Good morning, Honey," I blurted in words slurred by my swollen, numb tongue in a deformed mouth. "You are just in time. I *'gottago'*! Jesus just left after putting life back. I'll try to walk by holding on to you."

I saw my feet touch the floor as I slid over the edge of the bedside rail. They were numb and bloodless. At that second a Bible verse raced into my mind: "I give you dominion over *all flesh.*" With a crooked smile I parted my torn lips and spoke gruffly: "In Jesus' Name: Feet, feel!" It worked instantly, and I stood up only to realize that I had no idea of how to walk. (My memory-bank was blank as regards how to walk!)[12]

Desperately holding on to Maybelle as she explained that I should put one foot at a time ahead of the other, we wobbled around the room, laughing at the sight we would make if anyone were around to see us. On the third round I could stand alone so I shuffled into the bathroom, just in time!

Once back in bed with Maybelle's help, I re-attached the several wires and needles and I spread out on the bed as the corpse had lain earlier. I had her ring for the nurse. A hazy figure appeared in the doorway too scared to speak. "Nurse," I whispered in a labored voice, "How soon may I go to the rest room?"

Almost in a scream, the answer came back: "You're a dead man. Don't try to scare me like that!" I did not see her again. She may have resigned that morning.

****

Jesus wanted me to laugh some more sometime later when my heavy lids parted as a dark-clad figure leaned against the bed. Without moving (since my body hurt all over) I peered through "waterfall-eyes" at a stooping figure with a Roman collar as he shook a liquid onto me from a little bottle. Mustering all the strength in my chest, I whispered: "You must be a Priest?"[13]

The extended arm jerked back and he straightened in shock: "Yes, the Chaplain!"

"Oh, thank you, Father; what are you doing?"

"I -I -uh, I'm giving you the rites of the Church."

"Thank you! I hope that you are using Protestant water," I said with an attempted smile.[14]

In shock (thinking that his holy water had indeed raised a corpse) he panicked and dashed for the door. "Wait!" I called out to him, "Why are you leaving?"

He spun around, stepped back and leaned with his face nearly on mine. (His color looked ashen as mine.) "I'm going to light a candle in the chapel," he shakily explained.

"Thank you, Father! Would you make it Baptist tallow? You see, I just came back from Heaven." This time his flight carried him out of the room. I felt better already as a verse had just popped back into my mind: "A merry heart doeth good like a medicine." (I chuckled, realizing that I must have this *one* verse memorized correctly!)[15]

My charming young Chaplain returned daily to inspect *his* miracle. I so enjoyed watching his daily progress in relaxing around a bloodless body. In my mind's eye I could better picture now the utter shock and pandemonium nineteen centuries ago when frightened bystanders had unwrapped "dead Lazarus" and heard him speak! This Chaplain, fresh from seminary, with a bottle and a candle, would not forget his first miracle for sure![16]

END NOTES

1. John 14:13-14; John 14:27; Isa. 26:3; Mal. 4:2; Isa. 57:18-19 **2.** I Sam. 22:29 **3.** Exod. 15:26; Ps. 147:3 **4.** Ps. 139:12; Ps. 14; Col. 1:11-13 **5.** II Sam. 22:36-37; Ps. 135:6; Rev. 4:11; Matt. 17:7-8 **6.** Gen. 8:20-21 **7.** Ps. 139:1,23; Heb. 4:15-16; John 5:39 **8.** Ps. 85:8 **9.** Jer. 9:24; Prov. 8:8-9; II Tim. 2:15 **10.** Luke 7:14-15 **11.** Matt. 9:5 **12.** Gen. 1:26; Ps. 8:6 **13.** Luke 6:21; Ps. 126:2 **14.** Ps. 126:2 **15.** Prov. 17:22 **16.** John 11:44-45

Question #11

"WHAT ABOUT THAT PERFUME?"

Lying weak and battered in a a hospital room awaiting transport back to California I realized that healing takes time especially when the Lord has left some tissues to be replaced. I was to remember that St. Paul called *his* resulting aches and pains a "thorn in the flesh!" Jesus left me my share as a daily reminder of His caring Presence throughout any trial.[1]

I clearly recall, on my second day, that the hazy form of a white-suited man entered and sat at my bedside: "I'm Dr. Clark—," he coldly announced. "You're a dead man. No blood in you; can't give you any; State law, you know, forbids transfusing a corpse. Blood is too scarce to waste. I don't know why the H---- you seem alive, but quickly tell *me* anything that I should tell your wife before you're gone."

"Really Doctor," I replied softly through swollen lips, "Jesus has told me I will live. My wife knows that already!"

He jumped to his feet in disgust. "G-- D-- it, they told me you were a physician not an idiot!" He turned away and headed toward the door muttering so I could hear him: "Any doctor knows that science has proved there is no God. Well, you're dead anyway, like your God."[2]

The Answer: "S.S.S."

Weeks later in my California bed, I was eager to learn about that perfume which filled my Paradise. It must be discussed in His Book! Maybelle read the passages which described how Jehova "distilled" altar smoke into "sweet-smelling savors" of obedient worship. Today, He distills our worshipful prayers! Both the sacrifices and the prayers must be offered from surrendered, obedient hearts according to His Will and His recorded commands whether written to us before or after the Cross![3]

The Scriptures Explain The Savors

Before the Lamb came to earth and shed His own blood, God had accepted burning sacrifices as obedient acts of repentance. But *after* the Cross no animal sacrifice was adequate! It was an abomination! Instead, Jesus prescribed fervent prayers (in His Name) directed to the Father Jehovah as our obedient act of seeking His forgiveness.[4]

The Scriptures reveal that Jesus' death on the Cross replaced God's temporary demand for animal sacrifices, since the Lamb of God was *totally* righteous. Therefore, God now regards our prayers as the prime evidence of our obedience towards Him. Since our imperfect minds fail to express perfect prayer, the Holy Spirit of God winnows our intents and transforms our speech into a heavenly language which become (to our ears) "groanings that can not be uttered" (being only understood by God).[5]

We are told in the Scriptures that God so highly prizes these evidences of worship (Old Covenant burnt offerings or New Covenant prayers) that He converts each into a "Sweet-Smelling Savour" stored in golden vials in the Throne Room! These then become the "sacrifices of praise" from our lips. Since heavenly creations are eternal (timeless), these sweet-smelling savors will last forever, filling the third Heaven with God's perfume. That indescribable aroma is what I had enjoyed in Paradise. I call it "S.S.S."[6]

(In direct contrast to Heaven's pervading perfume is Hell's unquenchable stench! I later found it so nauseatingly horrid that it can not be described. The presence of demons in Hell (the place of spiritual death [separation from God]) saturates it with their rotten, decaying fumes! Jesus described them as "unclean spirits." That they are, in every sense. Even our noses are given the ability to discern between pure and putrid spirits!)[7]

In the Book God lovingly explains that "whatsoever...is pure" deserves our thoughts and becomes our goal: all else is a stench! "Avoid it, pass not by it, turn from it, and pass away!"[8]

I read what the Book says about "S.S.S.":

1. **Moses**, the Wilderness Wanderer, has this to say:

   Genesis 8:20-21: *"And Noah built an alter unto the Lord; and took of every clean beast and of every fowl, and offered **burnt offerings** on the altar. And the Lord smelled a **sweet savour**; and the Lord said in His heart, I will not again curse the ground anymore for man's sake; for the imagination of man's heart is evil from his youth; neither will I again smite anymore every living thing as I have done."*

2. **King David**, the Psalmist, describes prayer and worship:

   Psalm 141:2: *"**Let my prayer be set before Thee as incense**: and the **lifting up of my hands** as the evening sacrifice."*

3. **St. Paul** understood that believers' gifts please God; his friends in Phillipi had sent him some to supply his needs:

   Phillipians 4:18b: *"...the things that were sent from you, an odour of a sweet smell, a sacrifice acceptable, well-pleasing to God."*

4. **Peter** disclosed that born-again believers please the Father:

   1 Peter 2:5: *"Ye too as living stones are built up, a spiritual house, a holy priesthood, to offer up spiritual sacrifices acceptable to God by Jesus Christ."*

5. **Christ Jesus,** the Lamb of God, became the ultimate Perfume:

   Ephesians 5:2: *"Walk in Love, as Christ also hath loved us, and hath given Himself for us as an offering and a sacrifice to God for a sweet smelling savour."*

6. **Paul** assures us: believers in Jesus Christ are sweet savors!

   II Corinthians 2:15: *"For we are unto God a sweet savour of Christ, in them that are saved, and in them that perish; to the one we are the savour of death unto death; and to the other the savor of life unto life."*

7. **St. John** in Heaven saw an amazing vision of prophecy:

   Revelation 5:8: *"And when He had taken the Book the four beasts and four and twenty elders fell down before the LAMB, having everyone of them harps and golden vials full of odors which are the prayers of the saints."*

Rev. 8:4: *"And the smoke of the **incense** which came with the **prayers of the saints** ascended up before God out of the angel's hand."*

A Fringe Benefit of Searching Scriptures

The search which Jesus had suggested in order to learn about "S.S.S." perfume uncovered other answers too! As I had searched for one answer others were found. As Believers discover, this is how Jesus (Yeshua) out-maneuvers our tunnel-vision in order to show us "a better Covenant" than we could ask for![9]

The "better Covenant"reveals an understanding of God's *timing*. We learn that He withholds some answers to test our *trust* (the exercise of faith). Others He withholds because an immediate answer would be inappropriate to produce a perfect result later. Most of our faulty and selfish prayers, if answered as uttered, would lead to ever greater problems. So many prayers are unsuitable, not discerning that our "need" is really some form of "lust" (selfish desire).[10]

Is is easy for man to forget the "size" of God Almighty and the immensity of His omniscience, and especially His immeasurable Love. So many prayers sound like acts of a puppeteer pulling strings and demanding instant answers. Our God sits on His Throne in eternal timelessness, seeing both *causes* and *results* at the same instant. He answers accordingly! In love, He assigned the Holy Spirit to do our praying for us (upon our request). Jesus says to seek our Father's Will *first* rather than our own.[11]

Despite some teachings in this "new age" ("spiritual arrogance") which substitute man for God, The Book nowhere condones man's assumption of "dominion" over Jehovah, the Great I Am! We are invited "to come boldly before the Throne of Grace," not to sit on it! Satan tried that once; he was cast down and out. It was a fatal mistake. Instead we are admonished "to ask...seek, and knock." We are to accept *God's* thoughts and answers because His wisdom and judgments surpass ours every time.[12]

I also found an answer to a personal puzzle: Why in Paradise had Jesus suddenly let me remember Maybelle, and had sent me back to earth? I discovered interesting answers in His Book.

END NOTES

1. II Cor. 12:7; II Cor. 1:3-7 **2.** II Pet. 3:3; Ps. 10:4,7; Ps. 14:1; Jer. 9:23-24; Rom. 8:7-8 **3.** Rom. 15:4; Gen. 8:21; Exod. 29:18; I Sam. 15:22-23 **4.** Col. 2:14; Heb. 9:12: Heb. 5:8-9; James 5:16; Matt. 6:6 **5.** II Cor. 2:15; Rom. 8:26 **6.** Exod. 24:5-7; Eph. 5:2; Rev. 5:8;8:3; Heb. 13:15 **7.** Matt. 10:1; Rev. 16:14; Heb. 5:14: Ezek. 44:23; I Jn. 4:1-6 **8.** Phil. 4:8; Prov. 4:15 **9.** John 5:39; I Pet. 1:10-11 **10.** Heb. 8:6 **11.** John 14:16-17; Rom. 8:26 **12.** Ezek. 28:2; Isa. 14:13; Rev. 20:10

Question #12

"CAN PRAYER AFFECT GOD'S PLANS?"

Yeshua had told me in Paradise that He was responsible for placing the sudden thoughts in my new mind about Maybelle, but He did not mention WHY. My search of His Scriptures reveals much evidence that certain prayer in fact permits Jehovah-God to change His mind! It is called INTERCESSORY PRAYER. He recommends it because His nature seeks it from any children whose hearts trust Him.[1]

These following Scriptures helped me to better comprehend the importance and impact of INTERCESSORY PRAYER.

What The Book Says About It

I. "Seek ye the Lord *while* He may be found. Call upon him *while* He is near. For My thoughts are not your thoughts, neither are your ways My ways, saith the Lord. For as the heavens are higher than the earth, so are My ways higher than your ways, and My thoughts higher than your thoughts."[2]

Interpretation: *Before* it is too late, start asking Me!

II. "Oh the *depth* of riches of the wisdom and knowledge of God! How *unsearchable* are His judgments and His ways past finding out. For who hath known the Mind of the Lord, or who hath been His counselor?"

Interpretation: Expand *deep* study before getting answers![3]

III. "And the *Spirit* of the Lord fell upon me and said unto me: Speak...for *I know* the things that come into your mind, every one of them."[4]

Interpretation: Expect the Lord to be *ready* to answer!

IV. "But the Comforter, who is the *Holy Ghost*, whom the Father will send in My Name, he shall teach you all things, and bring all things to your remembrance, whatsoever I had said unto you."[5]

"Likewise, the *Spirit* helpeth our infirmities: for *we know not* what we should pray for as we ought: but the Spirit Itself maketh *intercession for us* with groanings which cannot be uttered, And He (Jesus) that searcheth the hearts knoweth what is the mind of the *Spirit because* he maketh intercession for the saints *according to the will of God* (the Father)."[6]

Interpretation: Pray any way, anytime, anyway! Our indwelling Spirit will *correct any mistakes* in our petitions or worship.

****

V. "Jesus answered and said unto him [Jude] 'If a man love me he will keep my words: and My Father will love him and we will come unto him and *make our abode with him.*'"[7]

"I am the Vine, ye are the branches: He [God] that *abideth* in me and I in him, the same bringeth forth much fruit: for *without me ye can do nothing.*"[8]

"I have called you *friends*, if ye do whatsoever I command you. Ye have not chosen me, but *I have chosen you*...that ye should go and *bring forth fruit*...that *whatsoever* ye shall ask of the Father in *My* Name He may give it you."[9]

Interpretation: Our Friend Jesus promises fruit, *IF* we abide *IN* the Vine. He then guarantees God's assent, because it is *in His Will* already.

My search for answers was exciting: I was getting to know my Friend better through each verse of Truth. He asks that we seek Him *diligently* although no man's mind would be totally able to comprehend *His* immense *wisdom*. He states that He knows our problems *in advance* of our prayers, and has provided His *intercession* on our behalf! We are reassured of *fruitfulness IF* we stick close by "abiding IN Him"! Yet, I was looking for an answer to clarify *whether He ever "changes."* I set out to find an *additional* description of God's eternal *nature*:[10]

VI. "And fear not Me, saith the Lord of Hosts. For I am the Lord, I change not..."[11]

"God is not a man, that He should lie; neither the son of man that He should repent; hath He said and shall He not do it? Or hath He spoken and shall He not make it good?"[12]

"The gifts and calling of God are without repentance."[13]

"The LORD (God) hath sworn and will not repent: Thou (Yeshua) art a priest after the order of Melchizedec."[14]

Interpretation: Clearly, the *nature* of God can *not* change. righteousness and omniscience are immutable!

****

Is this then the end of the search? Not quite! His Word talks about a *Repentant* Father of Mercy:[15]

VII. "*If* that nation against whom I have pronounced, turn from their evil, *I will repent* of the evil that I thought to bring against them."[16]

"And *if* it do evil in my sight, that it not obey My voice, then *I will repent* of the good, where with I said I would benefit them."[17]

"*If* ye will still abide in this land,...I will plant you and not pluck you up; for *I repent Me* of the evil I have done unto you."[18]

****

"Then spoke Joshua to the Lord...and the sun stood still in the midst of the heaven and the moon stayed, until the people had avenged themselves...and there was no day like that before it or after it, that the Lord *harkened* unto the voice of a man: for the Lord fought for Israel."[19]

"Who can tell *if* God will *turn and repent* and turn away from His fierce anger that we perish not? And God saw their works, that they turned from their evil way; and *God repented* of the evil that He had said He would do unto them; and He did it not."[20]

****

"Then came the word of the LORD to Samuel, saying, '*It repenteth Me* that I have set up Saul to be King; for he is turned back from following Me, and hath not performed My commandments.' *So* Saul died, and his three sons...."[21]

"And again the *anger* of the LORD was kindled against Israel...and when the angel stretched out his hand upon Jerusalem to destroy it, the *LORD repented* him of the evil, and said...'It is enough.'"[22]

Interpretation: God clearly discloses to mankind that His unchanging NATURE includes both *mercy and anger*; these are ingredients in His *just judgments*. He alters *decisions* to *fit* circumstances! Only His *Laws* were fixed in stone, not His *LOVE*! He *is* the ONE GOD WHO CAN LOVE SINNERS![23]

****

An Illustration

The following account tells *the story* of ancient evil times when God elected to change His Mind! The anguish of God's heart shows through this pain-filled decision He was *forced* to make. It foretells that He saw you and me "down the line" by sparing Noah; we *too* could experience His grace much later.

VIII. "And God saw that the wickedness of man was great in the earth, and that every *imagination* of the thoughts of his heart was *only* evil *continually*. And *it repented the LORD* that He had made man on the earth, and *it grieved Him* at His heart. And the LORD said, I will *destroy man* whom I have created. *But* Noah, found *grace* in the eyes of the LORD."[24]

Explanation: the above list of illustrations (along with many others) makes the answer very clear: although God's *Divine NATURE* can never change (nor would it ever need to). His *Divine Verdicts can* change! Although "God is the same yesterday, today, and forever" as regards His PERSON, yet *HIS Book* reveals that *He can and does change His METHOD OF OPERATION* to fit *changing* situations![25]

****

God Does Listen To You And Me

That is when PRAYER comes in. Yes, *PRAYER CHANGES THINGS.* God *is* moved by it. His *Hands* are *set free* by *our* prayers to accomplish *His Will*, His Words are *set free* to accomplish their goals. His Spirit is directed by the Father to convey the *answers* (yes, no sometime) and, to explain (teach) them to the petitioner![26]

That is why Jesus prayed and taught His disciples to follow His example. That is why He was upset at their failure to pray with Him at least "for an hour" before His arrest. That is why St. Paul repeated the admonition to "pray without ceasing." That was Paul's reason for praying behind his prison bars all night. *God does hear.* He does react. He even alters His *procedures* when His *prior* approach failed to "get the job done" (only because we did not listen or wait).[27]

Once we have prayed and listened and learned, Jesus says, "GO and Tell!"[28]

END NOTES

1. II Tim. 2:15;23-24 **2.** Isa. 55:6,8-9 **3.** Rom. 11:33-34 **4.** Ezek. 11:5 **5.** John 15:26 **6.** Rom. 8:26-27 **7.** John 14:23 **8.** John 15:5 **9.** John 15:15b-16 **10.** I Tim. 2:5; Heb. 12:24 **11.** Mal. 3:6 **12.** Num. 23:19 **13.** Rom. 11:29 **14.** Ps. 110:4 **15.** Isa. 16:5 **16.** Jer. 18:8 **17.** Jer. 18:10 **18.** Jer. 42:10 **19.** Josh. 10:12a,13a,14 **20.** Jon. 3:9-10 **21.** I Sam. 10-11; 1 Sam. 31:6a **22.** II Sam. 24:1,16 **23.** Ps. 136; I John 3:16; John 3:16 **24.** Gen. 6:5-7a; Luke 17:26-27 **25.** Heb. 13:8 **26.** John 6:38; Isa. 55:11 **27.** Luke 22:44; John 5:30; Matt. 26:40; Acts 12:5; I Thess. 5:17; Acts 16:25; Deut. 12:28,32; Mark 7:14 **28.** Matt. 28:19-20

Question #13

"DOES INTERCESSORY PRAYER WORK?"

Weeks later I searched as to why Jesus had sent *me* back to earth! *Someone* must have prayed: yes, several (besides my praying wife, Maybelle).[1]

From various sources I had discovered that a lovely black housekeeper next door in Chicago had been about to hang up the laundry in her backyard when the horrible sounds of my cracking body came across the fence. She screamed, looked over the fence at the body dangling by its feet with the head in a puddle of blood, and dashed to her phone. Her first call alerted the ambulance; then her frightened voice informed her pastor:

"Pastor Brown, please help! The man next door just fell to his death. Tell our Prayer Line to pray for his lovely wife. She needs help *right now*."[2]

Thus was started a chain of events which would include other prayer lines in the matter of minutes. YESHUA listened as voices implored:

"Jesus, You are Lord and You are the Resurrection and the Life! You said so. Please raise up this man's body down at the hospital. His wife needs him. *We believe* that You can do miracles *now* like you did for Lazarus. Now we'll do *our* work down here while *You* do a miracle! Thank you for being our Savior. Amen."[3]

****

I must assume that YESHUA was overjoyed to see so much *faith*! He must have decided even while He and I were busy walking and talking in Paradise that He would honor those prayers. I was *available* to be sent back as *proof* of His power over death and of His love for anyone who believed His Book enough to *ask*![4]

Indeed, I was the unworthy recipient of this most fantastic proof that *prayers* work, even when spoken by or for strangers. My life was being changed as were Jesus' plans, *by prayers* which had leaped the distance between earth and Heaven![5]

Answers From The Book

YESHUA had already told me where His answers can be found: "Didn't You Read My Book? *Search* the scriptures for in them you will find the truth!"[6]

Sure enough! I found the answers about prayers which do change events and people. They are in The Book. God even tells us *His* thoughts so His children can understand amazing truths about using His prayer line today...[7]

    I.   Who Can "Dial" God For Answers? (Friends)

        "You are *My friends, IF* you do what I command you. No longer do I call you servants, for a servant does not know what his Master is doing: but I have called you friends, things that I have heard from My Father *I have told you.*"[8]

    II.   Why Would God Answer? (Love) (His)

"For God *so loves the world* that He gave (gives) His only begotten Son that whosoever believes on (into) Him should not perish but hath everlasting Life."[9]

III. What Is The Answer? (Gifts) (His)

"*Whatsoever* ye shall ask the Father in My Name, He will *give* it unto you. Hitherto you have asked nothing in My Name; ask and ye shall receive, that your *joy* may be full."[10]

IV. How Is That Possible? (Faith) (His)

"*Have FAITH* in *God.* For verily I say unto you, that whosoever shall say unto this mountain, Be thou removed and be thou cast into the sea; and *shall not doubt* that those things which he saith shall come to pass, he shall have whatsoever he saith."[11]

V. When Is The Answer Received? (Now)

"Therefore, I say unto you, Whatsoever things you desire, *when you pray, believe* that you receive them, and ye shall have them."[12]

VI. Why Is An Answer Not Received? (Lust)

"Ye lust, and *have not*; ye kill and *desire to have*, and *cannot obtain*: ye fight and war, yet ye have not because ye ask not. Ye ask and receive not, because ye *ask amiss*, that ye may consume it upon your *lusts* (idle pleasures)."[13]

VII. What Is The Bottom Line?

"Let not your heart be troubled: ye believe in God, *believe also in Me!*"[14]

****

Now I had my answer: I was back on earth *because* my wife and unknown friends of Jesus had turned to God. They "let go and let God." He was thrilled, they were thrilled, I was thrilled! He was blessed, they were blessed, and I was blessed![15]

I became their living illustration of the power of intercessory prayer; an "unbelievable experience," in fact! I immediately wondered who else in this age of Grace had reported any similar miracle? It must be "in The Book!" And it is! I re-read the account with breathless excitement. A Jesus-hater called Saul had been chasing down "believers" to have them imprisoned and killed. One day he held a youngster's coat (Stephen's) and proudly watched the other haters murdering the youth with stones. As Stephen gazed upward at Jesus sitting in Heaven, Saul leaned over him for a closer look into the dying eyes. He was stunned to see an inner glow of glory. It shook his self-righteous soul. Had this young man really seen Jesus on a throne? The truth became fact a few days later as Saul faced the blinding light of Jesus, and repented: "Lord, WHAT WILL YOU HAVE ME TO DO?" We know that Jesus changed his name to Paul, and Paul trudged the known world for YESHUA![16]

I knew that St. Pauls letters would tell me *more* about this limitless power called "intercessory prayer." I noted that he too had been stoned to death at Lystra for claiming that Yeshua was the Loving, Living Messiah! He (like me) had been caught up into Paradise and had seen and heard unbelievable, indescribable truths about Heaven. I rushed to read his inspiring words about *prayer* which YESHUA had taught him during his quiet retreat into Arabia prior to his visit to Paradise.[17]

This is what St. Paul had to say after Jesus had taught me about "INTERCESSION":

"I exhort (you) that, first of all, supplications, prayers, intercessions and giving of thanks, be given *for all men*; for kings, and for all that are in authority; that we may lead *a quiet and peaceful life*; in all godliness and honesty. For this is good and acceptable in the sight of God, Our Saviour."[18]

Then Paul further states his own dedication:

"*Without ceasing* I make mention of you always in my prayers."[19]

"Brethren, *my heart's desire and prayer* to God for Israel is that they might be saved."[20]

"For this cause also we...*do not cease to pray for you*, and to desire that you might be filled with the knowledge of His will in all wisdom and spiritual understanding...being fruitful...strengthened in all might...giving thanks unto the Father."[21]

"I thank God...that without ceasing I have remembrance of thee *in my prayers* night and day."[22]

****

The prophet Isaiah had already foretold one of Messiah's ministries (upon which St. Paul would later expound):

"(The Messiah) made *intercession* for the transgressors."[23]

St. Paul stated very bluntly his unshakable reliance upon Jesus' *dependable* intercession for us before the Father:

"It is Christ that died, yea rather that is risen again, Who is even at the right hand of God, who also maketh *intercession* for us. For I *am persuaded* that neither death nor life nor angels, nor principalities, nor powers, nor things present, nor things to come, nor height, nor depth, nor any other creation (created thing) shall be able to separate us from the *love of God*, which is *in* Christ Jesus, our Lord."[24]

The writer of HEBREWS nails down the evidence of Yeshua's authority to be our Intercessor:

"But this Man (Jesus) because He continues forever hath an *unchangeable* priesthood."[25]

"Wherefore He is able to save them to the uttermost *that come unto God* by *Him*, seeing that He *ever liveth* to make *intercession* for them, For such a High Priest became us, Who is Holy, harmless and undefiled, separate from sinners, and made higher than the heavens...the son Who is consecrated *forevermore*."

"We have not an High Priest which cannot be touched with the feelings of our infirmities; but was *in all points* tempted like as we are, yet without sin."[26]

St. John reaffirmed Jesus' role in our behalf:

"If any man sin, we have an *advocate* with the Father, Jesus Christ, the Righteous: and He is the propitiation (reconciliation) for our sins; and not for our sins only, but also for the sins of the *whole world*."[27]

****

St Paul now tells us the most *astounding truth* that a believer can absorb! *Only the Almighty God* of LOVE could share *His own* Spirit *to do our praying for us*! God told Paul to tell us:

"Likewise, the *SPIRIT also* helpeth our infirmities (weaknesses): for *we know not what to pray for as we ought*, but the Spirit itself maketh INTERCESSION *for us* with groaning (fervent gushings) which cannot be uttered (put into words). And He (Jesus) that searcheth the hearts knoweth what is in the Mind of the Spirit, because He (the Spirit) maketh INTERCESSION for the saints *according to* the Will of God.... What then shall we say to these things? If *God* be for us, who can be against us?"*[28]

James, the half-brother of Jesus, wrote confidently:

"If any of you lack wisdom, let him ask of God that giveth *liberally*...but let him ask in *faith*, nothing *wavering*."[30]

In *Hebrews* we again read:

"Let us therefore come *boldly* unto the throne of grace...and find help in time of need."[31]

****

Truly, the BOOK itself testifies with awesome adequacy to the abundant love of Jehovah God *through* Jesus Christ from Whom the Holy Spirit today provides answers to faithful prayers!

Does prayer change God's mind? The answer has been told: prayer actually re-aligns *our* minds to conform with His! From our point of view, He seems to change; but our prayers actually change *us*. As we pray, we actually draw nearer to His Throne of Grace, and our mountainous perplexities fade in the brilliance of His Face![32]

Does prayer change our needs? Every praying believer knows that answer! As we approach the Throne, the size and

---

*This *searching question* is only resolved by one *honest* answer: "me," "us," "ourselves"! Let anyone who may be timid about approaching the Throne Room of our majestic Intercessor, *know this*: He has known about *your* problems all along, even *before* you did. And He *is* your comforter! Let not our "timidity" rob us as we pray![29]

nature of our burden seem to lose immensity and importance. When we finally allow His finger to touch our load, things change: not God's position, just His posture; not our petition, just its purpose! As Jesus leans forward, we see in one hand a scar; in the other His answer prepared *in advance* for a *better* result than our puny requests could have deserved.[33]

We hear a loving, gentle Voice, assert: "Trust Me, My child. My thoughts for you are more in number than the sand."[34]

St. Paul's conclusion sums up the whole need for our placing trust in the Everlasting Adonai of the scriptures:

"If God be for us, who can be against us?"[35]

Having resolved that question, the Book tells us to "occupy" (Greek for "go to work," "get busy")! Once the Lord has "tooled up" His worker to "go-and-tell Good New first to the Jew, then to the Gentile, then to the ends of the earth," His promised mercy and grace start following with "signs and wonders."[36]

I was to find that out for myself.

END NOTES

1. Phil. 4:6; John 11:41 **2.** Acts 4:24,30 **3.** Matt. 18:19; Phil. 2:3-5 **4.** Matt. 8:10,13 **5.** I Tim. 2:1-2; Ps. 34:17-18; James 5:15-16 **6.** John 5:39,47; Matt. 22:29 **7.** II Tim. 3:14-17 **8.** John 15:14-15 **9.** John 3:16 **10.** John 16:23-24 **11.** Mark 11:22-23 **12.** Mark 11:24 **13.** James 4:2-3 **14.** John 14:1 **15.** Ps. 103:1-4 **16.** Acts 9:1-31; Gal. 1:13-16 **17.** Acts 14:19-20; II Cor. 12:1-9; Gal. 1:16-20 **18.** I Tim. 2:1-3 **19.** Rom. 1:9 **20.** Rom. 10:1 **21.** Col. 1:9-12 **22.** II Tim. 1:3

23. Isa. 53:12b **24.** Rom. 8:34,38-39 **25.** Heb. 7:24-26,28b **26.** Heb. 4:15 **27.** I John 2:1-2 **28.** Rom. 8:26-27,31 **29.** II Tim. 1:9-10 **30.** James 1:5-6 **31.** Heb. 4:15-16 **32.** Rom. 12:2 **33.** Matt. 11:28-30 **34.** Ps. 139:17-18 **35.** Rom. 8:31 **36.** Luke 19:13; Acts 1:8

Question #14

"A MILLION PEOPLE: REALLY?"

In His Book Jesus emphatically repeats that *His* Omniscience in eternity permits Him to know *us in advance* of our being born! He has laid out our paths and numbered our days while preparing answers to problems as yet *unencountered*. To crown His *parental obsession* for our welfare throughout our journey among tares and thorns and persecutions He further promises never to "leave nor forsake" His children. Then He *seals* their names in the Book of Life![1]

I Was An Available Illustration

At all times Jesus knew my weaknesses better than I. He knew the future which His path for me would encompass. He foresaw that a medical career for me would become a busy traffic pattern of intersecting dilemmas. Before pushing me into medical arenas and public forums He must lead me into solutions to my timidity and fear of people and crowds. It would take years, but His plan would work! (That is part of His know-how!)[2]

As A Youth

My boyhood problem was IMPATIENCE. In my case He chose to teach me through music. He arranged for the BOYS

CLUB to donate to me the use of a battered, antique French Horn in Jr. High School. I was so proud of it. My teachers and Band Master said to "learn the notes." But God wanted *me* to appreciate the "rests." Someday I would need to understand.

It turned out that no melody is perfect without its "rests." It is the *pause* that refreshes. The brain needs a moment of quiet to appreciate the grandeur and extent of the subtle statements being projected from strings or reed! Each rest is a silent *lesson in living*, a cure for impatience! Even our mud-bodies need time to refuel, and our fatty brains need quiet times to reflect. *Patience could result* once I applied the lesson that *God's* music has rests: Satan's does not![3]

Music then became my "mixer" with people and crowds. It is God's number one method of communicating. I found myself invited into dozens of bands and orchestras and church groups to "blow my horn." God was curing my fear of people as a *fringe* benefit![4]

Some sixty long years later God intended that I be tested as to how well or poorly I had learned His lessons about REST and PATIENCE while I was physically on the shelf recovering from the shock of returning to earthly existence. After tasting the ecstasy of Paradise with Jesus I became fretful. I begrudged the new aches and altered senses which my numbed nerve-trunks began to transmit as they were restored. I disliked the wasted time "sitting around like a patient." Pastors and friends largely avoided me; they felt uncomfortable in my presence, not knowing whether to congratulate me or to sympathize over my "still being around!" At best they would venture to ask "How are the scars doing?" I was getting the "REST" for sure; but not much evidence of PATIENCE.[5]

My impatience mounted for the next five years. Maybelle and I prayed and prayed that the Lord would open doors for us to be again useful, then show us the next step to take. Even the "Spirit within" seemed silent.[6]

One morning the doorbell rang.

Since I had left already to admit a patient for surgery, Maybelle blindly felt her way to the front door and spoke through the crack: "Who is it?" (Pause) "Your friendly Avon Lady. Do you need any supplies today?"

"No thank you," replied Maybelle in her sweet voice. "By the way," she added, "I have something for *you* if you wish to talk with me. I can share what *Jesus* can do for ladies to make *them beautiful*! Do you know Him?"[7]

"Oh yes! He's my Savior," came the excited response. "You are the first person who has ever asked me about Him! I'd love to share Him with *you*!"

God *had* answered! He opened a literal door for two ladies to meet and greet. And He opened our *door of opportunity* to start a ministry of telling others about the Love He has poured out for all to share with Him.[8]

In fact, the rest of the story is worth the telling: God may do something similar for you. Ask Him!

In answer to Maybelle's query as to her visitor's knowledge of any local Church where the Holy Spirit was *welcomed* as Comforter and *Guide*, the Avon Lady recommended a tiny Calvary Church whose fiery Armenian Pastor relied upon the Spirit for messages and resulting salvations. Three days later we visited the one-room "sanctuary" on a prayer meeting night, and sat in the back row. A guest speaker, unknown to us, mounted the small podium. He stated that the Spirit had just told him to cancel his prepared message in favor of devoting the entire evening to "words of knowledge and edification" for *each* member present! Maybelle and I exchanged glances, wondering "What goes on in this place?"[9]

Without hesitation the speaker's finger pointed at me and Maybelle, as he broke the silence: "Will the gentleman and lady in the back row please stand? The Holy Spirit has a word for You!" Hesitantly we stood, wondering again, "Is this service for real?"

He continued: "I do not know who you are, but the Spirit of God does! He says to inform you that you will soon be speaking to millions of people about your experiences a while ago. Thousands of persons will be led to the Lord through your ministry." As he quoted corroborating verses from the Bible, his wife jotted them on a piece of paper which is still in my Bible today.[10]

I could scarcely await the end of the service to tell him how impossible such a "word of knowledge" would be in my case. "My hospital and clinic duties fill every day," I explained. "You must have picked the wrong person for your prophecy tonight!" He just smiled, unimpressed. "Wait on the Lord," he added. Another wait? Enough is enough, I thought as I turned away.[11]

The Phone Call

A few days later a phone call interrupted a rare moment of eating at home. "This is Paul Crouch of Trinity Broadcasting Network," I heard a pleasant voice say. "Are you Dr. Eby who visited Calvary Church awhile ago? My former seminary classmate just called to say that he met you and suggests that you should be heard over our TV network? Would you be willing to tell your story?" I hesitated, but he prevailed.

God's Answer

Just as our 3-hour Praise-The-Lord program ended, a phone counsellor rushed up with "a praise report hot off the wire" from a lady who had just listened to my "amazing story of Jesus' love for lost souls." Two hours *before* the program she had loaded her 45-calibre pistol to commit suicide and end a life of prostitution and drugs. To "see one last TV program" she had flicked across the dial, stopping abruptly at "40" where the speaker was explaining: "Hell is horrid, but *Jesus* died to save *you* from it!" That was a Name new to her. She laid down her pistol, dialed the station, and accepted Him as Lord![12]

I turned to Paul and asked: "How many people watch this program?"

"It could be three million tonight," he estimated. I remembered suddenly Calvary Church and "words of knowledge!" God had ended my drought. He would use me now![13]

END NOTES

1. Ps. 103:17; Ps. 139:15; Isa. 65:24; Jer. 1:5; II Tim. 2:13; Gen. 28:15; Heb. 13:5 **2.** II Cor. 12:9; Ps. 23:3; Prov. 3:6; Jer. 1:8 **3.** Eph. 6:11-14; Rom. 5:3-4 **4.** Ps. 150:3-5 **5.** I Cor. 2:9-10; Rom. 11:33-34; Ps. 38:11 **6.** Luke 18:1 **7.** Job 40:10 **8.** Ps. 91:14-15 **9.** Acts 6:3; John 16:33 **10.** I Cor. 12:1,8 **11.** Jer. 1:6-7 12. Jer. 1:9; Jude 23 13. Matt. 19:25-26

PART THREE

DIALOGUES WITH JESUS ON TOUR OF HELL

Question #15
"YET A LITTLE WHILE?"

Although I have elsewhere in former books recounted my awesome encounter with Jesus 1977, when He intercepted me in Lazarus' Tomb, it again requires inclusion here. I condensed His conversations with me in those early books because of my limited time and energy. In these subsequent years the impact of *our* meetings and *His* intentions in these final days require a more complete recitation of His loving words.

Any trip to Israel involves the unexpected! Our first trip (Maybelle was then with me) was no exception. When our bus stopped at Bethany, I elected to descend the two stories below ground-level into Lazarua' Tomb, never guessing that my tour was about to be "re-routed" that day![1]

Squeezing through a narrow slanted tunnel I emerged along with two other tourists into an eight-foot-square cavity hewn from the original cave where Lazarus' rotting body had lain once for four days awaiting Jesus' command to "Arise!" The guide shouted after us: "Take a look. Mooof along, pleece. Others want in!" Suddenly the single light bulb went out, and we were in *total darkness* underground![2]

Startled voices from the stairwell above added to the sub-dued cries of my "tomb-mates" who suddenly disappeared while I was dropping to hands and knees to grope blindly for the exit. Then I was alone, in silence, bathed in heavenly light such as Jesus emitted when I was in Paradise five years before! Instantly I realized that He must be near, and there He was, standing beside my kneeling form. I nearly exploded with excitement. His partially plucked-off beard was noted as I looked up. But first I saw the golden hem of his garment from which ten toes protruded. Then I sensed the permeating profusion of His heavenly love. I leaped to my feet, noting a golden sash and wide glowing girdle. I looked into the eyes of YESHUA! His left arm encircled my shoulder. He grasped my arm with steel-like strength. At His touch my mind became again the Mind of Christ which I had experienced in Paradise. Immediately He spoke: "My son!" then paused a moment for me to realize that I was again in a spirit body. What a Voice! No words can adequately describe it: sovereign, merciful, authoritative, all powerful, infinitely keen and cutting yet meek, gentle, and lovingly mild! His words seemed like controlled *thunder* flowing from His radiant face encircled by illuminated golden locks which brushed His shoulders with their curling tips.[3]

"My son," He repeated, "I have much to tell you, and many things to show you! You are to *Go Tell Them! Tell Them! Tell Them!* I have brought you here to reveal to you My commission for which you have been praying since I showed you Paradise. *I am returning soon* to receive My Body of believers, and I want you to tell people about those things I showed you in Heaven and the things I am about to show you in Hell. I want you to tell them about the choice they must make between Me, the Master-Creator, and Satan, the master-deceiver and murderer. I will return for you and My Body of Believers before you can complete this commission! I am returning *soon!* I could not release you to tell about Paradise until I had shown you Hell as it *now* exists."[4]

I recoiled at the thought. "But Jesus, You saved me from Hell when I made You my Lord! I don't want to even see that place. Why me?"[5]

Again that exquisite Voice, mind to mind: "*You* are available! The time is short. I need eyewitnesses of heaven and hell to convince lost souls that they must use their free will to choose a Master to serve, here and hereafter. There are but two Masters, Satan or Me. There are but two families, the family of Satan or the Family of God. There are but two places after death to spend eternity: in Hell or in Heaven. I need you *today* as an eyewitness to the reality of both!"[6]

Jesus gave me no time to reply. With lighting-like speed He began a review of the Law and the Prophets under the Old Covenant, and His eyewitness autobiography of His suffering and death on the Cross. He ended with His description of the coming events when He would rid an unrighteous world of its blatant sin, thus permitting His righteous reign over all nations! His voice became excited as He painted mental pictures of His final victory over Satan, and His new heavens and earth without any taints and curses from Satan's presence.[7]

His eyes, all this time, blazed with *lazer-like brilliance* of love, power, and righteousness. They kept my attention riveted on His face, just as His words etched into my mind the glories of His plans and the terrors which He had suffered in order to be the Slain Lamb for mankind's sins. Never can I forget His graphic portrayal of His trial and crucifixion when His "image was so marred" by Roman beatings that His Father had turned His face away from that Cross in horror, and the mobs and disciples ran away in fright. Nor shall I forget His recalling His three days of preaching to the captive souls in Sheol. His joy seemed to mount as He related to me how His Father had arranged for *Him* to speak to *every* departed soul that they had created since Adam, and to display His nail-pierced hands and feet and riven side! Not one soul was being omitted from hearing and seeing the *promised Lamb of God* who had just paid their ransom with His own blood! Jesus said that He led a "host" of believers forth from Sheol into Paradise. He had just prepared to receive them, in the third heaven.[8]

He paused, as thought to rivet my attention upon His next statement: "I want you to go tell them, My son, that I shouted 'IT IS FINISHED' when I finally released My Spirit back to My Father. Tell them that *I was not kidding!*"[9]

Momentarily I felt stunned at the Lord's reference to "kidding!" It seemed so unlikely a choice of words for Him to be using. Then I remembered another moment five years earlier when in the hospital room HE had spoken to me out of His Shekinah Glory Cloud saying "With your hands you will heal!" I had heard myself reply "You must be kidding!"

And now, five years later, Jesus was holding me in His tight embrace, and reminding me again that He was *not kidding* about His intent once and for all to restore and redeem sinners at the Cross, nor about restoring me to life, nor about giving me a new commission. I would have collapsed to my knees in adoration and awe at this evidence of His personal reassurance to me were it not for the strong left arm around my shoulder. Nor could my eyes loose from His gaze into them. Again He spoke:[10]

"I have more to tell you, My son. You will not complete your commission for Me before I return for you and My Body of Believers. I am coming that soon." Instantly a near-blinding golden light appeared behind me. Instinctively I turned my head. On the Tomb wall, being written without hand or brush, were appearing these words in beautiful English script.

THERE IS YET A LITTLE WHILE
BUT VERY LITTLE!

From each letter, drops of glittering gold "paint" were falling to the floor and exploding into a transparent gold Cloud that filled the tomb! I gasped and looked back into Jesus' face. The Cloud was of the same material as the small one which had entered my hospital room when Jesus had spoken from it to me, a corpse. I was overwhelmed![12]

"Fear not, My son," He quickly reassured me, "I want you to have a visual memory of My promise to return soon. It will help to sustain your faith during times of testing that lie ahead. You are to go *tell them* about your experience in Paradise when I let you die five years ago. Now I must show you Hell for two minutes. You must *tell them* that you have seen both. I will cast you in the role of an unsaved sinner, but I will send my Mind with you to answer questions. You will not see Me while in Hell. I will erase you name for two minutes from My Lamb's Book of Life, then replace it when you are returned here."[13]

I reacted like a knee-jerk! "But Jesus, I don't want to go to Hell! You said that believers won't go there! How is it that You can send me to Hell and bring me back?"[14]

A gentle but sad Voice replied: "Do you forget that I am Lord? I went to Sheol *in person* long ago and took the keys of Hell and Death from Satan's grasp. I can, and will, let you experience the terrors of Hell as it now is; and I will restore your name to the Book of Life upon your return. You will be *an eyewitness* to what Satan has planned for those who *willfully* ignore or reject My free gift of Eternal Life! There is *so little time* left for you and others to tell the Good News of Salvation around the world. Fear not, I go with you now in My mind, but not my body."[15]

The Present Hell - A Holding Tank

Instantly I was in the center of the earth, the most indescribable plunge of terror that can be experienced. I was standing in a cavity in solid stone just large enough for me and a legion of demons: Ice-cold, ink-black, totally silent (as we on earth know sounds). I screamed to God, then realized that no one could hear me. I was totally isolated from Him, as a sinner, for two minutes of hopeless terror![16]

Suddenly Jesus was speaking to my mind. The pit of Hell became "illuminated": I was seeing now with spirit eyes! My feet were surrounded with a thousand tiny demon-forms like spiders whom suddenly I could hear taunting me in obscene language, all their own. Horror gripped me.[17]

Total Horror

Jesus was saying, "This is the *true* Hell in this Age of Grace. When the old Sheol was emptied, the reprobate unbelievers became *isolated* from God here (as they desired) until the Great White Throne Judgement which I will show you in a moment."[18]

Jesus' "moment" seemed an eternity! In this age of God's grace, when punishment of sin is being postponed until the Great White Throne Judgment 1000+ years from now, the total isolation from God's peaceful Presence is *total* terror. I can not describe the horror of being cooped up with death-dealing demons. It is total panic. Jesus had caste me for two minutes in the role of an unbeliever who had died without accepting the gift of salvation. No form of isolation can be as terrible as separation from the Almighty God who gives all good things to the just and the unjust! The demons around me in that tiny hole in solid rock were ecstatic at my desperate wish to escape. They thought I had really died![19]

"You blankety-blank fool!" they screamed at me (mind-to-mind). "You listened to our lies up on earth, and we got you now! You can never escape from us. Satan assigned us to deceive you, and you listened! We know about the Lamb of God; He would have saved you from us, but you wouldn't listen to Him. He would have taken you to Heaven, but you wouldn't believe Him. Now we'll make it hell for you forever, you — - — idiot!"

(I have cleaned up the above taunts. Actually, their language was so loaded with obscenities and filth that it merits only complete removal from human ears.)[20]

The worst was not over. With their fiery eyes fastened upon me, the one thousand spider-sized demons suddenly jumped away from my feet onto the side walls of this rock-hole, racing up around my head. Their screaming taunts were audible upon my mind as separate voices, all declaring my profound stupidity in selecting hell instead of Heaven for the rest of eternity. Their constant shrieks of insane laughter over my plight were accented by their chants of AHA! AHA! AHA! (apparently a demonic AMEN!).[21]

As if signaled by an unseen conductor, this legion of filthy fallen angels suddenly dropped to the rock floor and ringed around my feet again. Deafening decibels of heavy-metal voodoo sounds filled the place competing for loudness with the thousand voices of frenzied *rock-&-roll bodies* in epileptoid seizures! Mimicking every imaginable obscene gesture until they were coupled in a mass of hysterical arachnoids, the demons taunted me. Wild gestures of invitation urged me to join their screaming "fun." "Our pit" echoed with every debasing word and phrase known to Satan's crowd.[22]

I screamed back at them: "You filthy demons. YOU! Who taught you this musical garbage and obscene writhings? Stop it! Right Now!"[23]

In unison the noise and motions ceased. In momentary silence they fixed hateful fiery eyes on me, then sneered "AHA's."[24]

"You'll get used to it, you fool! You'll never get out of here. Our boss, Satan, bound us in here just to keep you here and to make it hell for you. He taught us *rock-sex-music* to use around the world to *destroy* the kids. It works. We have deceived the minds of almost all children already. They think that smut is the best fun. They think that lust and sex are signs of growing wise. We have them believing that anything goes as long as it defies the notion of a living God. They prefer devil-worship; they think it is more exciting. We deceived them, and they don't know it yet. Just wait!" They were rollicking with raucous laughter at the mere thought.[25]

"Why do you unclean spirits remain in this stinking hole when you could spend your time in the sunshine and fresh air?" I demanded.

A cloud of hatred seemed to chill their reply.

"You idiot! Don't you know? You could read! We are the first creatures in the universe to be deceived by Satan! He fooled us angels. He said he was the real God. We followed him instead of Jehovah. Now we are chained, as it were, in this Hell-hole. We are not allowed to leave because we were assigned to get you here, and we must keep you here. We hate Satan but we cannot be saved because Satan cannot save anybody. You human beings have a choice of a Leader on earth, either Jesus Christ of Nazareth or Satan the deceiver. You fool: you could be in Heaven right now if you hadn't refused Jesus' offer of Life!"[26]

Suddenly their invisible "conductor" seemingly tapped his baton. The deafening heavy-rock beat began as the spider-chorus resumed its epileptoid convulsions of sexual writhings to obscene demonic language and laughter.

Just in time I was lovingly snatched from this pit of Hell. I could have gone stark raving mad from terror had it lasted any longer. (But Jesus was merciful to me!). Suddenly I was standing before the *Great White Throne* in awful terror. Obviously this was some portion of Heaven, but my fear mounted. I felt naked in body and soul and without a friend to plead my case. I felt dirty, and without merit.[27]

Then Jesus again spoke to my mind: "As an unsaved sinner you are now before the Judgment Throne. You will witness the wages of sin. Watch and listen closely."[28]

A White Throne of Justice

I gasped. This was to be the ultimate moment of terror from which I had been saved before this unexpected tour to Hell. At this split-second Jesus allowed me to sense a flashback to my glorious joy at having been saved (until a few minutes ago when He erased my name from His Book of Life). The contrast was devastating! *Then* I was loved: *now* I was lost![29]

It loomed in front of me, a great White Throne emitting its heavenly light. A huge Person sat enshrouded in a mist-like Cloud. Again I gasped at the awesomeness of this moment. I was beholding *Jehovah's Presence*, the Great I AM, as any sinner (unbeliever) must who has elected to be judged for his works rather than for his faith and trust![30]

I wanted so badly to see His face. I was sensing His *Love* and *Power* which seemed to be blasting through the envelope of mist which obscured His eyes. I blurted out: "Jesus, I must see *God's* eyes. Yours were so full of love in Lazarus' Tomb; His must be glorious!"[31]

On my mind, an instant answer: "My child, in your present form it is impossible to look upon Jehovah-God and live. You are here to be instructed and shown the eventual judgment for sin. In My Book the penalty is called 'wages of sin,' known as *death.* You are being shown that God's righteous *justice* demands that He prevail over the works of Satan, whose deceptions are accepted and acclaimed by rebellious mankind. You are not to be destroyed here, but simply given an eye-witness proof that a time and place of Judgment has been already prepared. You must Go Tell Them back on Earth what you saw here!"[32]

The Lamb's Book of Life

Out from the misty envelope which shrouded the majestic Figure extended a hand holding an *opened* Book. A second hand emerged to flip the pages with lightning speed.

Again the Voice: "The Almighty God is searching for your name!" It was not there. (My two minutes were not yet up.)[33]

I noted the title of the Book inscribed in Hebrew on its back cover: *LAMB'S BOOK OF LIFE.* Although I screamed out toward the Throne "My name must be in there," I knew it wasn't. (Never does a lost sinner care about God or His "Book"!).[34]

The search was finished! The Book was slammed shut with a thunderous noise. I shuddered. A Voice from the Throne majestically declared:[35]

"THIS IS *OUR* FAMILY ALBUM. YOUR NAME IS *NOT* IN IT. THERE IS ONLY ONE OTHER FAMILY—THE *FAMILY OF SATAN*! DEPART!"[36]

Jehovah pointed beyond me to the most heart-rending sight ever to be seen by unsaved rebellious creatures. He spoke:

"Be cast into the Lake of Fire; it is THE SECOND DEATH, prepared for *your* father the Devil, and *his* angels."[37]

Terrified, I saw the galaxy-sized caldron of leaping flames. Mercifully, I was snatched back into Lazarus' Tomb. I had seen enough! For several nights I could not sleep for seeing again the sights of Hell. Then I prayed to be freed from the *terror* of those memories, and Yeshua obliged. He restored His Spirit of power, love, and a sound mind. I was His "son" again! Hallelujah! My name was back in His Lamb's Book of Life![38]

END NOTES

1. Deut. 32:8-9; Deut. 34:4 **2.** John 11:39 **3.** John 1:5,9; Rev. 22:5; John 16:16,22; I John 1:5; Isa. 50:6; Eph. 3:19; Rev. 12:5; I Cor. 2:16; Gen. 3:8; Isa. 66:6; Ps. 29:3-4; Num. 6:5 **4.** Matt. 24:44-51; I John 5:11-13; Matt. 6:24; Matt. 23:8-10; John 8:44 **5.** I John 3:14 **6.** Acts 16:30-31; John 3:16 **7.** Matt. 5:17; Matt. 26:56; Luke 24:27;44-46; Rev. 21:1,4 **8.** Rev. 1:14b; Isa. 52:14; Matt. 27:4-6; Psa. 68:18; Eph. 4:8-10; Col. 2:15; Titus 2:11; Eph. 1:20-23; II Cor. 12:2-4 **9.** John 19:30; John 17:4 **10.** Ps. 89:13; John 1:12; John 11:25; Acts 1:8 **11.** Matt. 24:30-31; Rev. 22:20 **12.** John 14:19; Acts 1:9; John 16:16,19 **13.** Titus 2:13; James 5:8; John 16:33; I John 3:3 **14.** Ps. 28:1,3 **15.** Eph. 4:9-10; Rev. 1:18; Rom. 5:15-16; Rom. 6:23; John 16:16 **16.** Matt. 22:13; Isa. 14:15; Isa. 38:18; Mark 5:9; I Sam. 2:9; Ps. 88:4-7,16; Ps. 115:17; Ps. 94:17,23 **17.** Rev. 20:1-3; Ps. 18:28: Ps. 139:12; John. 1:5; Mark 5:8-9; Mark 1:34 **18.** Luke 13:28 **19.** Ps. 88:14-16; Luke 21:27; Job 33:22,24 **20.** Acts 8:7; Matt. 23:33; II Pet. 2:4; Ps. 88:4,6;

Mark 3:11 **21.** Mark 5:8-9; Ps. 40:15; Ezek. 36:2 **22.** Deut. 32:17-18; II Sam. 22:31-32 **23.** Matt. 10:1 **24.** Ps. 40:15 **25.** Matt. 8:29; Deut. 32:31-33; I Tim. 4:1-2; John 8:44-45; Deut. 32:19-26; Matt. 17:14-21 **26.** II Pet. 2:4,9; Luke 4:41; Jude 6; Matt. 10:28; Matt. 25:46 **27.** Luke 8:27-29; Rev. 20:11-15; Dan. 7:9-11 **28.** Rom. 6:23 **29.** John 15:11; Rom. 5:11 **30.** Ps. 96:13; Ps. 97:6,9 **31.** Exod. 33:21-24 **32.** Exod. 3:6; Exod. 33:20; Rom. 6:23; Ps. 19:9; Matt. 13:40-43; Matt. 25:41 **33.** Rev. 20:12 **34.** Rev. 21:27 **35.** Exod. 32:32-33; II Sam. 22:14 **36.** I John 3:10; Matt. 7:23 **37.** Rev. 14:9-11; Rev. 20:14-15; John 8:44; Matt. 25:41 **38.** Ps. 94:17; I Pet 3:14; II Tim. 1:7; 1 John 3:1-2; Matt. 6:9; Rev. 21:27

PART FOUR
IT IS WRITTEN IN THE BOOK

Question #16
"BREAD FOR HEALING?"

After my return to active practice, the Lord began to open doors of opportunity to fulfill His command to GO and TELL. Initially through Christian television exposure a mounting number of invitations to share my testimony about Heaven and Hell provided week-end "training" sessions for me. For me it was a new means of communication that I faced from public platforms as compared with the one-on-one conversations in an office and hospital setting![1]

A disturbing question began to nag me after months of ministering to hurting bodies and minds and souls in prayer lines. It had been an age-old question, long before my time, yet now it directly affected *me*! Oppressed people were repeatedly asking: "Doctor, why did my healing last year wear off, after an evangelist prayed over me and I felt well?" He quoted Jesus' Word that believers could 'lay on hands' and the sick people will recover.[2]

I, too, needed a better answer than I had received from so-called divine healers. So I went to the *Source*, my Healer!

At my bedside for many nights I posed this question (about failed or temporary "healings") in humble petition for answers. I "reminded" the Lord that He in person had commanded me to GO TELL THEM to choose Him as their Savior and Healer. I "refreshed" His memory that He had promised (as He put life back in my body at the hospital) that He would use my hands through which to heal others. I had obeyed. Some were healed, others not. Some stayed healthy, others not. Jesus, the Creator and Repairer, must have smiled, or frowned, knowing that the answers were already in His Book![3]

His answer was not what I was expecting. Instead, I kept sensing a persistent "small voice" urging me to write a book in which I was to share the story of His love now! He was "reminding" *me* of *His* personal, attentive care over the many years while my parents and family had sought His wisdom and guidance: truly, a succession of Divine *touches*! "My son," the Voice whispered, "I gave them for you to share, not hide! I can bless others through your testimony *now*. I will select the experiences which I gave you for teaching or testing purposes. *Write* them to help others!"[4]

Frankly, that idea did not fit my schedule! Repeatedly I countered with excuses: too busy, unskilled as a writer, ignorant of ways to publish and distribute a book, unaware of which episodes God would have me select, never wrote a book before, etc., etc.

Again God must have smiled. The Voice persisted:

"My son, why be disobedient? My Spirit will select the material. I will provide readers and audiences to acquire the book. Now do it *for Me!*"[5]

****

During weeks of "one-finger typing" in my only free-time from midnight till 3 or 4 A.M., I was praying for guidance as to what to write next. As usual my tired mind swayed like a pendulum between drowsiness and excitement while it reviewed the memories of encounters with Jesus, His unseen touches of protection and providence. Questions about the amazing healings which I was seeing as we traveled and shared the Good News comprised much of my prayer time.[6]

My Lesson

One night my typing was abruptly interrupted by my hands suddenly becoming "frozen" in mid air above the keys. I could not move them. For a moment I was fearful of disc collapse. Then a voice behind me softly spoke:

"RICHARD!"

Reflexly I replied, "Yes, Honey, I know it's late. I'll finish this page first, then I'll get some sleep!" (My Maybelle was accustomed to enforcing her house-rule that I sleep at least two hours before breakfast!) I turned to smile at her, but no one was there!

I gasped: it was not Maybelle's voice at all. In shame I blurted out, "Jesus, forgive me; what do you want?"[7]

His answer started an amazing conversation:

"My son, I want you to read My *sample prayer* which I gave to My disciples when they asked Me how they should pray. I have something to tell you."[8]

In typical *human* pride, I replied, "But Jesus, I have that prayer memorized!"

"Certainly, I know that! I said for you to *read* it!"

Instantly my useless hands "unfroze" as He spoke, and my right hand reached for the worn Bible on the shelf. In a flash I remembered how Jesus' own prayer had illustrated how to talk *with* the Father rather than just "saying." It was heart-service rather than mere lip-service. Quickly He spoke:[9]

"My child, you have asked Me to clarify questions about My so-called Divine Healings. You have seen them apparently 'wear off.' You searched My Book for answers but missed them. Now, start reading!"

Silently I rationalized, "This is unreal. It can't be happening. Is my question *that* important?"[10]

Out loud I replied: "Is it alright, Jesus, if I read one phrase at a time? You can stop me wherever You wish to explain the answer you have for me." I sensed His assent this time, and I started reading:

OUR FATHER WHICH ART IN HEAVEN(pause)
HALLOWED BE THY NAME(pause)
THY KINGDOM COME(pause)
THY WILL BE DONE(pause)
ON EARTH AS IT IS IN HEAVEN(pause)
GIVE US THIS DAY OUR DAILY BREAD. (STOP!)[11]

"What does this mean to you, My son?"

"Well," I hesitated, "It is a petition for nutritional needs, just as your disciples relied upon you for fishes, corn, bread, or figs day by day."[12]

"What did I tell them to ask for?"

"You said, 'Daily bread,' Lord."

"Now you have your answer! In My Book you may have read about 'bread' without remembering that *I* am the Bread of Life in the *Kingdom* of God. That is why I told you to pray that it come to Earth! My body is the Bread *broken* for man's healing. The breaking symbolizes my Blood washing away the sin that caused all the trouble since Adam. In My Book I tell you about *Manna*, the food of angels in Heaven, which I shared with my fretful people in the wilderness! It was only good for *one* day, except over the Sabbath when prayer and thanks were offered. That prevented *decay!* Do you get the point?"[13]

Yes! Suddenly it was clear: Jesus *is* the Bread of Life. Only HE is essential for *healing* the physical or spiritual breakdowns in His creatures! Its preservative? Praise and Thanksgiving! Its longevity? One day (without Praise and Thanksgiving). Its nature? Supernatural. Its purpose? Mercy. Its properties? Those of Jesus, the example of Love. How had I missed the deeper meaning of that prayer after saying it all these years? I must be sure that I have it right now.[14]

"Jesus, if I understand correctly, You are saying that as 'Bread' You heal. Therefore the rules about Manna apply to healings? Without daily praise and thanksgiving the healings disappear? *Worshipful* prayer maintains the repairs that You have given as Your reward for obedience and faithful trust? Is that why St. Paul urged us to maintain a constant attitude of prayer? Is that why King David declared the 'praise shall be continually on my lips?'[15]

I heard three words of reply, then Jesus left my room:

"NOW YOU KNOW!"[16]

****

Only the glow of sunrise aroused me hours later in time to dash to the hospital to scrub for surgery. When the patient's anesthetic had worn off, I told her how to maintain her healing! Not by paying her bill, not by thanking her doctors, not by lauding some pills: God *expects* that anyone would do that. What really *excites* The Healer is a daily uplifted heart and hand conveying Praise and Thanksgiving to His Throne Room. He says so![17]

END NOTES

1. Matt. 10:8; Acts 5:15-16 **2.** Mark 16:18 **3.** I Pet. 2:24; Gen. 1:27; Isa. 53:5 **4.** Rev. 1:19; Heb. 2:2; Isa. 30.8 **5.** Matt. 10:20; Ezek. 3:27; Titus 2:15 **6.** Ps. 30:5; Ps. 4:8; Ps. 5:2-3 **7.** John 10:27-28 **8.** Matt. 6:9-13 **9.** John Ch. 17 **10.** I Tim. 2:5 **11.** Matt. 6:9-13 **12.** Luke 24:41-43; Mark 2:15-16 **13.** John 6:35,45; Exod. 16:20-21; John 6:31,50;Exod. 16:24 **14.** John 6:50,56 **15.** Ps. 116:17; James 5:16; I Thess. 5:17-18; Heb. 13:15; Ps. 34:1; Ps. 150:6 **16.** Gal. 1:12 **17.** Ps. 100:4

Question #17

"DO I UNDERSTAND YOU RIGHT?"

An ancient adage suggests that "the proof is in the pudding." As months rolled by, I pondered Jesus' parable to me about healings. It was so important that I should remember Him correctly. My own body was steadily being repaired of its multiple damages, but not yet completely. Perhaps it would be a perfect subject for an experiment! I decided to put it to the test.[1]

Testing My Own Healing

I cannot forget what happened! Of course I first talked to Jesus. After all, He is my Chief of Staff! "Dear Lord Jesus, It has been months since you and I discussed healings. I *must be sure* that I understand Your teaching about daily praise and thanksgiving for the Bread of Life which is You. Please check me out! Starting this morning I will omit from my prayers any reference to my bodily healings of my remaining aches and pains. I will see what happens! You know that I love You no matter what trouble I get into (if I am right). Then I will thank You for putting me back in running order!"[2]

That first day (I called it Day #1) nothing unusual occurred. I went about my daily rounds at the hospital and clinic without detecting any new discomforts or disabilities.

On Day #2, I awoke aching. I prayed before arising, as usual, and asked the Lord's blessing upon others, not me. When I tried to get up I discovered that my legs were stiffened, my arms tingled as though frost-bitten, my vision blurred off and on, and my mind seemed to have blank spots! Breakfast tasted flat and my "innards" felt queer. I spent a "poor day" at the office! That night it was hard to get comfortable in any position. Sleep was fitful at best.

Day #3 was worse. I could not arise or walk. Eyelids twitched, waterfalls like falling tinsel ringed my vision; the room turned cartwheels when I bent over. The pulse was erratic, and the bowels cramped. My damaged spinal discs again compressed the nerves, shooting agonizing fires and crampings into all my muscles. I crawled slowly to the bathroom and back to bed. Maybelle brought some food(?) but it tasted and felt like warmed-over leather. I cancelled my office schedule from the bedside phone. I still decided to tough it out. No *praise* today![3]

I did wake up on Day #4, but I felt barely alive. My eyes saw only shadows around the room and through the window. I could not move legs or arms. My mouth was numb. My ears were ringing with thousands of discordant bells making hearing impossible. I was a basket case. My heartbeats were too weak to feel. I breathed faintly, and tried to speak to Maybelle, but she shook her head in disbelief, and tears started in her eyes.[4]

It was then that I realized I had not told her about my experiment. She obviously assumed that the Chicago doctors were correct at last: "Your husband may be alive now but his injuries will take him soon. Be prepared for heart or brain failure!" Right in front of her this morning she was watching it happen.[5]

It was her tears that jolted me as I saw a shadowy Kleenex lifted to her eyes. Silently I shouted:

"Jesus! The experiment worked, but I hurt my dear wife. Please replace the miracle that You did for me months ago. I thank and praise You for that marvelous recovery. *Right now*, Jesus, remove Maybelle's sorrow, and give her joy this morning! Then restore me quickly so I can go to work and can tell others for sure about the *holding* power of praise and thanksgiving! Hallelujah! Thank you for being my Savior day by day!"[6]

An hour later I was at work in my office, as fit as before. Again I could combine human therapies with "laid-on-hands" in prayer that *others* would know His love and power better. Yes, Jesus had meant what He said![7]

END NOTES

1. Matt. 7:20 **2.** Job 23:10 **3.** John 16:20 **4.** Ps. 86:6-7; Job 13:15; Ps. 22:11 **5.** Ezek. 13:3 **6.** John 11:41; John 16:22-24; Acts 3:6-8 **7.** Luke 5:25; Ps. 40:1-3

Question #18

"THE SAVIOR'S HEALING: IS IT FOR TODAY?"

We *can* enjoy the Divine Presence (the Spirit of God) right now, right here, on earth. This "newness of life" is the believer's indwelling "Love Letter" signed "From the Kingdom of God, Kindness of the Holy Spirit!" In fact, Jesus admonished His disciples to pray, "...Thy Will be done ON EARTH AS IT IS IN HEAVEN." (It is God's Will that *no man be lost!*)[1]

Incidentally, this healing from sin's presence, power, and penalty is *not* a "religion," nor is it attainable by being "religious." The Bible is the *only* valid source of Truth: it teaches that *God's healing* is the restoration of His intended relationship with His earthly *family*: He, the Father; they, the children. The process of finding one another HE calls "salvation." His gifts is "eternal life!"[2]

Salvation Is A Relationship

Salvation has nothing to do with "denominations," any more than does healing, whether spiritual or (less importantly) physical. This unique Father-child relationship required an *initial* horrible slaughter of an innocent Lamb, called "Yeshua" by the Father. His death would become the greatest ransom of all time, paid to buy back from Satan the souls of sinful man. Only one requirement would remain, the Bible explains: man must believe on that *Jesus*, the *Slain Lamb*, the *Only Name* under heaven which can save! That makes *salvation a gift* from God, not a reward for works![3]

That is where the *matter of healing!* comes in: it is a part of this renewed relationship which innocent, Holy, righteous *Blood* cements together to last eternally! Healing is not up for grabs to the highest bidder, any more than is Redemption. *Both are Gifts* from God of Mercy and Grace, and are available to the *meek* and *humble* who surrender pride and prejudice in order to seek *first* the Kingdom (citizenship) of God in place of vanity and sin.[4]

Despite "other gospel" teachings to the contrary, the Bible discloses only One God as the Healer. The Bible nowhere teaches us that anyone can command God to perform healings or miracles! We are His pupils, not His boss. We can USE His POWER, but never ABUSE it! We are His ambassadors but never His task-master. He invites us to work only *in His Name!*[5]

Endtime Precautions About "Entertainment Healings"

Numerous books are written on the subject of so-called Divine Healing and Divine Health. In these times it has become the fad and fashion of some groups in society to exploit the drawing power of *promises* of miracles to fill auditoriums with screaming onlookers. Such practice of "medicine without a license" requires adept balancing on a tight-rope between *fraud* and *faith!* The *God-given privilege* of utilizing *any Spirit-loaned gift* is easily abused and even violated.[6]

The Author of the Old and New Covenants laid down certain parameters to limit, and certain privileges to expand, our implementation of His gift of healing *power*. His Word carefully instructs us in the use of this POWER (Dynamos). Unfortunately, due to language barriers, His words are blurred all too often in the excitement of pacing a platform or "building" a ministry.[7]

It is not meant by this author-physician to disparage Spirit-filled Christians who are willing to be used by the *Holy Spirit* "as He leads." I do mean to discourage the blatant hysterical exhibitions of *staged* programs aimed at obtaining high ratings on someone's ego scale! Satan is using divers tactics (since he is a super-imitator, a non-tiring actor) to simulate healings, and even use musical "hypes" which precede them. In truth, we are now seeing deceptions and exaggerations and mislabelings which are indeed confusing newly-rooted believers in search of the *real* Messiah.[8]

If we doubt this fact, then we are already deceived. No warnings ring more clearly in the Bible than those directed to our "last generation" in this Age of Grace! Every writer in the New Covenant warns repeatedly about the end-time deceits of Satan. In fact, Jesus Himself climaxes these prophesies by calling *compromising* "Christians" "lukewarm" (like vomit which He is forced to spew out)! At the Judgment He calls them 'goats,' fit only for Hell.[9]

Certain "Healings" To Avoid

We must avoid "healings" being auctioned off to build a *following* for increased "ratings"! Healings are not rewards for "works," nor manifestations of superior "anointing." They are strictly *gifts* from a loving Creator to accomplish His will *in* a distressed child. They are given by the Father to *honor* His Son's obedience on the Cross, and to exalt the Holy Spirit who inhabits those children of God who request and accept such a "touch" from the Comforter! They are administered through any available "member of the Body" (submissive to the will of God) at such a time and place as God deems appropriate or necessary.[10]

Imitations Can Confuse

For the serious believer, *God's Book* lists *no one* but the Most High God as capable of performing *true* miracles or healings or redemptions. It readily *warns* us about imitation, deceptions and lies which the Adversary, Satan, uses all too effectively to bewitch and bewilder, to distort and destroy. Satan even suggests himself as the best choice for a god, and dares to imply that man can even order the Most High God to revoke His divine laws to fit the whims of the world's "life styles"! Yet the deceiver flees in the True God's presence when a believer *approaches* the Book's Author to donate *His* peace *in place of* confusion: "For God hath not given us a spirit of fear; but of power, and of love, and of a sound mind." St. Paul further admonishes us to make "full proof of [our] ministry" lest like others we "shall turn away...from the truth, and shall be turned to *fables*!" God's healing power is no fable; it is His gift for us to use with His guidance and approval![11]

Healings Last Through Praise

Jesus explained to me (while in Lazarus' Tomb as I related previously) that Healings only remain when *daily praise and thanks* to the Lord are given to Him regularly. As our Divine Healer, He fully merits our worship *every* day. As King David said: "Bless the Lord, O my soul, and *all* that is within me, bless His Holy Name. Bless the Lord, O my soul, and forget not *all* His benefits Who forgiveth *all* thine iniquities: who healeth *all* thy diseases!" Again it is written: "Give thanks unto the Lord; call upon His Name; make known his deeds among the people." David discovered his "secret": "I will bless the Lord at *all* times; His praise shall *continually* be in my mouth."[12]

END NOTES

1. I John 3:1-3 **2.** John 14:6; Ps. 37:39-40; John 10:10; Rom. 6:23 **3.** Rom. 5:8; Heb. 9:22; John 3:16; John 14:11-12; Mark 2:10-11 **4.** Ps. 49:6-8; Matt. 5:1-12 **5.** Exod. 15:26; II Tim. 2:15; Acts 5:29; Mark 16:15-18 **6.** Phil. 4:5; Prov. 12:5 **7.** II Chron. 21:18-19; Phil. 3:18-19; I Cor. 12:30; I Cor. 13:1 **8.** I Cor. 12:9-10; Ps. 119:104; Matt. 15:19; II Cor. 4:1-2 **9.** I Pet. 5:8; II Pet. 2:18; II Tim. 3:13; Matt. 24:24; Rev. 3:15-16 **10.** II Tim. 1:9; Eph. 2:9; Ps. 107:20; John 12:28; Rom. 8:9,26; James 5:16 **11.** Exod. 15:26; Jer. 10:10-13; II John 7-8; Isa. 14:14-15; Gen. 3:5; I Cor. 14:33; I John 3:7-8; II Tim. 1:7; II Tim. 4:4-5 **12.** Ps. 103:1-2; Ps. 105:1; Ps. 34:1

Question #19

"DO HEALINGS REQUIRE THE *CREATOR'S* POWER?"

Our *only* source of knowledge regarding *supernatural* healings is, of course, the Word of God. Our *only* source of such available Power to Heal is *through* The *Comforter* (Jesus' own description of The Holy Spirit's function). He was left on earth when the Risen Lamb ascended to Heaven's Throne Room. The *only* source of permission to use and display such healing Power is "Our Father Who Art In Heaven." To Him our humble and childlike requests are directed in the Only Name Given Under Heaven Whereby *we* may be saved and healed! *Jesus!*[1]

Jesus amplified His amazing teachings about ministry and healing powers after His resurrection. He wanted to make quite clear (to His disciples and to you and me) that God remains Sovereign over *all* gifts and power even after such gifts and power are bestowed or loaned to us. Never were we to be His servants except as we would act "in My Name!" His actions *through us* were *never* to become empire builders *for us*, but Kingdom-wonders *from Him!*[2]

Jesus admonished His followers during His six-weeks-stay on earth after the Tomb in solemn statements of hope and awesome promises too fundamental to ignore:

"...Jesus began to do and to teach until the day in which He was taken up, after that He through the *Holy Ghost* had given *commandments* unto the apostles whom He had chosen; to whom also He showed Himself alive after His passion by many infallible proofs, being seen by them for forty days, and speaking of things pertaining to the Kingdom of God..."[3]

"But wait for the *promise* (baptism of the Spirit) of the Father, which (saith He) ye have heard from Me...Ye shall receive POWER *after* that the *Holy Ghost* has come upon you, and ye shall be Witnessess..."[4]

And when it happened, the POWER of God's Holy Spirit fell upon them, inwardly and visibly, and they became his *first* Pentecostals.

"...they were with *one accord* in one place and suddenly there came a sound as of a rushing mighty wind, and it filled the whole house where they were sitting. And there appeared unto them cloven tongues like as of fire, and it sat upon each of them. And they were *all filled* with the Holy Ghost and spoke in other tongues *as* the Spirit gave them utterance.... Now when this was noised abroad, the multitude came together and were confounded.... But Peter said unto them...this is that which was spoken by the prophet Joel...."[5]

'And it shall come to pass in the last days, saith God, I will pour out My Spirit upon all flesh, and your sons and daughters shall prophesy...and it shall come to pass that whosoever shall call on the Lord (Jesus) shall be saved....'[6]

"Hear these words....

"This Jesus hath God raised up, whereof we are *all* witnesses; therefore being by the right hand of God exalted, and having received from the Father the *promise* of the Holy Ghost, He *hath shed forth* this (proof), which ye now see and hear."[7]

NOTE: An "end-time REVIVAL" can be the *result* of God's promise of an outpoured Holy Spirit *left here* upon Jesus' return to Heaven. After Pentecost's "fire"Jesus has continued to pour out God's *Infilling* Spirit upon believers who would accept this gift of His love. It was, is, and will be available during this Age of Grace and the seven years of The Tribulation of Nations while Jesus is ascended. Then He returns after a bloody Battle in Armageddon to reign as King of Kings at Jerusalem over the prophesied Kingdom of Heaven on Earth![8]

Healings Are Gifts, Not Obligations

Healings of body, mind, and soul are listed in God's Book as manifestations of God's gifts to His "re-born" children. St. Paul declares that God sees us believers as "new creatures (species) *in* Christ Jesus," no longer to be considered as Jews or Gentiles because we have become "new born" with God as our heavenly Father! "Old things have passed, and behold all things are become new. And *all* things are of God who hath reconciled us to (into) Himself by Jesus Christ!"[9]

New House Rules

Once we become believers (members in *God's* Body), there are *new* "house rules" to obey. His Book says so. No longer do we make our own rules and demand our "civil" rights and serve as our own boss. Instead, we are under His law only, the Law of Love! We thus become pilgrims on earth but *citizens* of Heaven.[10]

Jesus said it so simply: He reduced the exhausting laws of the Old Covenant into two commandments for us under the present New Covenant. These are His *new* House Rules for today:

"Thou shalt *love* the Lord thy God with all thy heart, and with all thy soul, and with all thy mind. This is the first and *great* commandment. And the second is like unto it, Thou shalt *love* thy neighbor as thyself. On these two commandments hang *all* the law and the prophets."[11]

A Healing Requires Submissive Love

The teaching is so clear: If we love Jesus, then we love also the Father *and* the only Holy Spirit! We *love* to be *in* His will by being obedient to it. Therefore when we request some kind of healing, our own will must become submissive (subject) to God's will. The Indwelling Holy Spirit of God can only honor a request for healing when it *aligns* with our Father's will. This includes the prayers of intercessors who "stand in behalf of" another person who cannot or does not align his/her will with God's. Our sovereign Heavenly Father must refuse to manifest a requested healing when it is not "in accord" with His Divine will! His love for us is too great for Him to grant an improper (lustful) request. He simply answers, "NO."[12]

Even for His Only Begotten Son the Father refused to remove "the cup of death," in order to permit Jesus to die for us! The Father was following His own House Rules: because with all *His* heart He willed that no man should be lost to sin without recourse to a Redeemer's Ransom. Greater LOVE hath no man! From sin to be healed would require the greatest *agony* that God The Father could ever endure. HE did that for you and me when He said "NO" in Gethsemane and, again when He momentarily forsook His Son Jesus bleeding on the Cross. *The*

Father's Gift to a perishing world was His ultimate SACRIFICE of Yeshua as His LAMB![13]

Jesus' gift of healing from sin's presence, power, or penalty is not a "religion" nor even something "religious!" It is *His manifestation* of *love*. It is His recognition of the re-established "Father-child" *Relationship* through a trusting belief in Jesus Christ. It is God's example of the Creator's caretaking! Only the *power* of and in the *Risen* Lamb can heal from sin or save from corruption! Obviously, only *THE* Creator can qualify as Messiah, the Yeshua.[14]

We must come to the logical conclusion (as revealed through the *Holy* Spirit and the *Holy* Scriptures) that "Divine healing" is God's Mercy as manifested through *His* LOVE! It is displayed at His selected times and appropriate places according to His magnificent *wisdom* and foreknowledge. It must be released in *conformity* with His established "House Rules" for *His* family's benefit, and to *His* honor and glory! He *alone* makes the choice of when, why, where or how He will *"supervene."* He *alone* can look ahead to determine that most effective method, modality, ministry, or means to employ. The manifestation is what *we* call a "miracle." *He* calls it simply "God-so-loves!"[15]

A further conclusion about this matter becomes also simple:

God *is* in the healing business (not the wealth business, as we might wish in our self-centered Wall Street mentalities)! Jesus warned: "Lay not up for yourselves treasures *on earth*...but treasures in Heaven!" Only *after* becoming "a humble, converted child," "abiding in Him," willing to "trust," "delight in," and "commit thy way" unto Him, only then can our souls "prosper" with heavenly blessings for use on earth! His Book says so.[16]

Rules For Qualifying

There are requirements to qualify for a miracle: from cover to cover the Book reveals them! Here is a simple checklist:

[   ] SURRENDER of selfish motives to God's Wisdom[17]

[   ] TRUST in God's Wisdom to provide proper answers[18]

[   ] OBEDIENCE to accept God's Sovereignty over Satan[19]

[   ] COMMITMENT to His decisions as a daily priority[20]

[   ] FAITH that Yeshua (Jesus) is the risen Mediator[21]

[   ] RESOLUTION to keep His Commandments as a loving child[22]

[   ] DAILY THANKSGIVING for His daily love and mercies[23]

Is it surprising therefore that God expects every "new creature in Christ Jesus (Yeshua)" to live by these standards as a *daily* walk? Whenever a believer does so, his miracle is automatic![24]

END NOTES

1. John 1:1-2,12-13; John 14:16-17,26; John 16:12-15; Acts 4:12; John 14:6,14 **2.** Acts 1:4-5,8; I Cor. 12:1-11; Rom. 15:18-19 **3.** Acts 1:1-4 **4.** Acts 1:8 **5.** Acts 2:2-4; Acts 2:6,16 **6.** Acts 2:17-18; Joel 2:28-32 **7.** Acts 2:32-33 **8.** Acts 17:6-7; Acts 1:5,8; Acts 5:32; Dan. 9:27; Rev. 19:6 **9.** I Cor. 12:9; II Cor. 5:17-18 **10.** Col. 3:12-15; Rom. 12:1-2; Phil.

3:20 **11.** Matt. 12:37-40 **12.** Matt. 26:39; James 4:15; John 6:38 Heb. 5:7-8 **13.** Matt. 27:46; John 3:16 **14.** Ps. 49:6-7,15; Matt. 9:1-8 **15.** Matt. 8:7; Luke 4:18; Mark 2:10-11; Matt. 13:15; John 9:1-3 **16.** Matt. 16:26-27; Matt. 6:19-21; Matt. 6:33; Matt. 18:1-4; Ps. 37:3-7; Ps. 1:1,5-6; III John 2 **17.** Job 13:15 **18.** Ps. 37:3 **19.** Rom. 6:17-18 **20.** Ps. 37:5 **21.** I Tim. 2:5-6 **22.** John 14:15-16 **23.** Col. 2:6-7 **24.** II Cor. 5:17; John 14:13-14

Question #20

"IS GOD CONCERNED ABOUT OUR DAILY FOOD?"

In stark contrast to today's food *fads* and diet *fantasies* the Bible reveals some oft-overlooked facts. After all, He created everything edible for something or some body to utilize along His *food chain*. He had it prepared and readied for each of His creations' immediate use. None of His flora or fauna, big animals or little ones, or mature man or eventual offspring could have survived their initial days on earth without foods of multiplied kinds. To have waited millions of years for "evolution" to discover and prepare a proper "breakfast" for each new species as it awakened on some given morning is patently ludicrous, not to mention insulting God! In fact God's Book sets the record straight by audaciously stating that He made and re-made presently living things in six days that had mornings and evenings long after He had put the sun in orbit! Until *He* re-writes His own Living Word, His children are expected to believe Him! Jesus declared it to be TRUTH![1]

His creatures were prepared for *His* pleasure to share and return His love with grateful praise for His majesty. This omniscient God established HEALTH as the normal condition for the first creatures which He made in His likeness. Mankind's food was a prime concern. Therefore God provided a multiplicity of foods to serve man's needs, no matter what part of the earth he might inhabit. Concurrently, God provided in Man's body a matching multiplicity of enzymes to handle digestive needs whenever man and food get together![2]

Being a *concerned* Parent, God used certain foods as object lessons to teach His "over-advantaged" children that He values *Obedience* as next to *Righteousness*! Foreseeing that His first couple would be "smarties" with unbridled liberty in The Garden, He selected *one* tree to be shunned by them lest its *special* fruit destroy their created Innocence. His loving plan failed: they snitched a bite, and opened the gate of disobedience through which Satan made his snake-like entrance into their minds and spirits. God then closed Eden to His rebellious "couple", ever after to be *downcast outcasts*, having lost their first "estate." They would even spawn a murderer as their first child, thus producing a *taint* that has spoiled every page of human history. (God has labeled it SIN!)[3]

Proper Eating Requires Obedience

Although it may seem quite illogical that God would link any demonstration of obedience to our eating habits, yet "it is written" that way in His Book![4]

God's very first test of Adam's faithfulness involved eating. Despite having "Divine Health" in *God's* image and body, a "perfect" Adam flunked the simple test! Being denied nothing else that looked good to eat in all of Eden, his *lust of eye* and taste buds forced him to bite into the only *forbidden fruit* in his fantastic world. God had said "Don't." Adam had reasoned "Why not?" Then Earth was no longer the same: Disobedience entered; Innocence fled! A just God cursed Satan and mankind.[5]

God had informed mankind that their menu would be vegetarian, without the shedding of blood, to insure longevity! For the few who followed that advice, their long lives became legendary. The rebels ate "whatever," lost touch with health and God, and finally watched a *floating* ark as *they* sank to oblivion in God's angry flood![6]

God's love began all over again with a "negotiated" menu! Mankind, now the carrier of disobedience genetically, would be allowed to shed blood but would have to atone for his sinning by repeatedly sacrificing animals *without blemish* as acceptable demonstrations of *obedience* to Jehovah-God. Rather than do that, mankind switched allegiance to man-made idols, until only one man remained loyal to the Most High God, his Creator. Refusing to lose more generations of man, God told His friend, *Abram*, to father a race of children, even at his old age! They would be special, peculiar, obedient, and zealous persons, chosen to *re-tell the news* of a Living, Loving Jehovah-Father. They would be God's nation, but would have to *eat and live* by God's house rules to succeed. Again they failed.[7]

This time a grieving Jehovah would "chastise" them, not by failed health, nor by a flooded earth, but by foreign captivities. Again God failed to get a faithful following. He tried famines and even predicted *more* discipline for His remnant of migrants from Hebron who languished in Egypt. Hunger did little to restore "God's chosen people" to proper worship.[8]

Now God tried His "trump card," called Moses! God disguised him as a true "King's kid" to give him prestige and authenticity in the great Palace. Once trained, Moses fled to the backside of the desert to take care of animals and talk to God as one "on fire" for His people. Moses got the message loud and clear to lead his people forth. Again Jehovah laid out a special *health* menu for His wandering Jews who must stay healthy for forty long years in a scorching desert![9]

Obedience would be their secret for success: *eat as ordered!* There would be clean and unclean food items to choose or reject. No overeating. Certain times of fasting and feasting. Obedience would finally get them to a "promised land flowing with milk and honey." Each tribe would receive apportioned land as its inheritance. *If* trustworthy, a mighty nation with an Eternal King would be *theirs forever* on a recycled earth where peace for man and animal would signal the *final victory* of the Lamb of God as the *ruling Messiah*. Manna, the "food of the angels," would enrich life with "no tears, no sorrow, and no pain."[10]

In the meantime during this age of Grace and Mercy God has declared a relatively open season on food selections. God originally assigned garden produce as man's menu for health. After sin entered the world, He permitted the eating of flesh. In the Sinai years He listed animals as being clean or unclean for food. (Jews bless their food to sanctify it for body use, both before and after eating it.)[11]

It is apparent that God's Book reveals both His *perfect* will in all human deportment and conduct as well as His *permissive* will. He could not act otherwise when His human family had become so utterly corrupted across the face of the earth. However, God's abundant kinds of foods (to satisfy the varieties of climates where they must grow) do not modify His overall rule that mankind must be "moderate in all things!" That rule includes *eating habits!* God has stated that "My people perish for lack of [all kinds of] knowledge." That covers both fleshly and spiritual shortcomings. In His Book we can discern "good," "better" and "best."[12]

For those who wish to approximate God's *perfect* will at the dining table, the Biblical outlines for healthy living remain understandable and available. For persons unable to afford "best foods" (due to poverty or drought or geography or wars) God, The Provider, shows His understanding by offering a *permissive* menu to handle sub-standard situations, but not without "dis-ease"!

And then there is prayer! History records both ancient and modern "miracles of prayer" involving *nutritional* answers in *emergent, exceptional crises.* God enjoys hearing from His children in need, whether too fat or too thin, too wet or too dry! His Book tells of all kinds of "helpers" available to Him. Whether ravens, quail, bees, fishes, loaves, manna, oil, water, or wine, Jehovah's arm of love has sent them in emergencies.[13]

Whatever God sets before us deserves our thanksgiving for His mercy. His Book says: "In all things give thanks!" "Seek His wisdom." Pursue "moderation in all things." "Feed the poor."[14]

Food is simply one evidence of God's loving providence. Why not invite Him as Honored Guest when breaking bread?

END NOTES

1. Gen. 1:29-30; Gen. 2:9; Gen. 6:21 **2.** Ps. 148; Ps. 150:6 **3.** Deut. 12:15-16; Gen. 3:3; Acts 27:34-36 **4.** Deut. 14:3 **5.** Gen. 2:16-17; Gen. 3:14-19 **6.** Gen. 1:29; Gen. 2:8-9; Gen. 6:5-8 **7.** Gen. 9:3-5; Lev. 11:1-47; Gen. 17:1-8 **8.** Ps. 106:40-43; Gen. 41:54-57 **9.** Exod. 2:10; Exod. 19:19-20; Exod. 2:12; Deut. 12:20-28 **10.** Lev. 11:1-47; Lev. 23:1-44; Num. 26:52-56; Rev. 19:6-7 **11.** Gen. 1:29; Gen. 2:8-9; Deut. 14:1-21; Matt. 6:31 **12.** I Tim. 4:3-5; Hos. 4:6 **13.** Mark 8:7-9 **14.** Luke 12:22-23; Eph. 5:20; Rom. 14:6

Question #21

"A VAN/THE CLOUD/THE VOICE?"

Perhaps my most amazing encounter with Jesus was some four years after my journey with Him through Hell! It was so unexpected and unique that only He could have foreseen the place and time, and prepared the participants without their realization. Only afterwards did the immensity of the miracle become apparent. I will try to share the memory of that day (which no words can adequately do).[1]

The *participants*: The Lord, Pat Robertson, the CBN van and young driver, Arthur Blessitt (who carries a cross around the world), a Piper Cub plane, and me.

The *occasion*: Pat's invitation that I be a guest on the 700 CLUB TV program again. I accepted. I purchased an air ticket to Virginia Beach but was unable to get a return ticket until the following day. It meant staying over a day, with no adequate explanation available.[2]

The *morning broadcast*: the Holy Spirit anointed the program by having very large numbers of people contact the counsellors with reports of salvations and healings; then He moved me to ask the studio audience if anyone needed physical healing. All did! The Spirit touched each one in rapid succession with evidence of healing. Pat was overcome by the Power in the studio, and retired to his study to recover (1 1/2 hours later) to address his convocation of employees.

The *afternoon events*: about 3 P.M. the young chauffeur of the CBN van tapped my shoulder (when Pat returned from his study to let me free to return to my hotel room). "You need food," he observed. I agreed. En route he told me that "tonight" would be the first time that his job had required his being up after midnight. "Tomorrow's speaker" had been unable to get a ticket into Virginia Beach and had hired a little Piper Cub pilot to land him here about 1:30 A.M. in a alfalfa field where the van would pick him up. The lad could not remember the speaker's name. Silently I asked the Holy Spirit to refresh his memory, while I reached across the van and touched his shoulder.[4]

"Oh," he exclaimed, "I remember now. The name is Arthur Blessitt, someone from Los Angeles who's been in Africa. Do you know him?"

"I certainly do. He's a favorite friend, but I thought he was in Africa for another month! I must meet him at the plane. He will be so surprised!"

The *reunion*: the lad and I watched as two pinpoints of light descended through the dark sky, and Arthur stepped out into the alfalfa field. I rushed from the van to welcome him. He turned gray in our headlights. In disbelief he reached to embrace me and nearly fell. I thought he was airsick. But no. He was overcome by some tremendous supernatural emotion. I asked, "What's wrong, Arthur?" Again he stared at me "Dick, it's a miracle! I can't believe it. You are really Dr. Eby, aren't you?"

Despite his buckling knees, I helped him into the van where he fell to the floor with his head in my lap. He was praying in intense fervor, saying over and over, "Lord, I can't believe this. I didn't expect it. You have done it. This is a miracle."[5]

The chauffeur headed through the field back to the highway. In the darkness of the van I suddenly heard a clear voice in my right ear, coming from behind us. I turned to see who it was that had commandeered a free ride back to town. No one was there.

The *next few minutes*: the van had now reached the highway, smoothly racing toward town. Quickly, I responded to the voice which had called me "Richard!" "It must be You, Jesus," I exclaimed in absolute amazement: "What may I do for You?"[6]

He replied instantly, in English, in the beautiful voice which I had heard in my Heaven and Hell encounters with Him! "My son, I have brought you here tonight to anoint Arthur to be, as I had promised him, like a second John the Baptist to announce to the nations that 'the coming of the Lord is at hand.'"

"But, Lord," I stammered in near shock, "I have no anointing oil!"

"I know that, My son. I give you the oil of the Spirit!"

"But Lord, I do not know the words to use in anointing so great a prophet in your behalf!"

"My son, I will put the words on your lips! All I need is your hand on his head. Do it for Me!"[7]

Just then Arthur twisted his head to look up at me: "Quick, Dick, do it!"

"Arthur," I exclaimed, "Did you hear His Voice? What did He tell you?"

"Jesus said that this is the moment when He had promised earlier to anoint me because 'the coming of the Lord is at hand.' I had refused that anointing years ago, but this is the miracle. DO IT QUICKLY!" He bowed his head again in my lap.[8]

I touched his head as I closed my eyes in the Presence of the Lord. From my mouth I heard Jesus' voice proclaim: "I hereby anoint you, Arthur, to be as a second John the Baptist to announce to the rulers of the world the 'Coming of the Lord is at hand'! Fear not. I am with you. This will be the final official invitation to the nations to return to Me. *I am coming soon! AMEN!*"[9]

Just then the van began to bounce and careen to one side. Instinctively I opened my eyes to determine why. The van was racing ahead on the graveled shoulder of the road, and had filled with a golden "fog" while Jesus spoke. I recognized it as the Shekinah Glory Cloud within which Yeshua in olden days appeared in the sky, temple, or mount. I gasped as I looked for the driver through it: and there he lay, slain in the Spirit, out cold, on the floor with hands above his head![10]

Frantically, I blurted out: "Jesus, turn off the motor!" In stunned silence I saw the dashboard ignition key turn to "OFF"; the motor coughed, and we came to a standstill only feet from a deep culvert. All was silent. How long? It seemed that there was no "time." Finally, the driver awoke, amazed and embarrassed. He struggled up into his seat, turned the key and we headed for the hotel in silence except for Arthur's steady prayer of praise for this "miracle." The Cloud left.

There is of course much more to this story. Arthur has told his part in his books and over TV. The "miracle" was that Jesus had brought the two of us together at a time and a place when neither Arthur nor I knew that we were on the same continent, let alone at the same alfalfa field! I knew nothing of the Messiah's promise to Arthur when months before in South America Arthur had asked Jesus during an encounter with Him on a dug-out boat to use *my* lips to re-affirm this announcement of His soon return. Had Jesus planned that the airlines would unwittingly cooperate by withholding air tickets from each of us on that very special day when He would again give Arthur this final commission?[11]

Comment

I personally need no more affirmation nor revelations of the "signs of the times" than those long ignored by people and nations since the prophets of old and the apostles after Pentecost proclaimed them for our edification *in the Holy Scriptures*. The Most High God, Creator of Heaven and Earth, has announced in *our* times that the "great *Day of the Lord*" is at hand.[12]

Why is this announcement important? Jesus has already proclaimed His answer:

> "For then shall be great tribulation such as was not since the beginning of the world to this time, no, nor ever shall be. And *except those days be* shortened there should be no flesh saved: But for the elects' sake those days shall be shortened...and they shall see the son of man coming in the clouds of Heaven with power and great glory."[13]

The loving Heavenly Father has tried for so long to get His children's attention. Let's start listening!

The Lord's Message: "Surely I Come Quickly."

I have shared this very personal experience for a purpose: namely, to discharge my responsibility to "Go Tell Them" that both the written Testaments and the rapidly emerging fulfillments of God's prophesies all say the same thing! In these final days before our Messiah *suddenly* returns for His Body of believers, He is frantically urging us to "look up, for your Redemption (Yeshua) draweth near!" (I am simply one small voice repeating what He said.)[14]

Amazingly enough, after thousands of years, millions of human creatures still elect to ignore the message. What is it?

Simply this: God loves His human family individually. He has a plan for each and for all collectively. He wants to salvage them from a sin-filled "life-style" by the blood-soaked sacrifice of His own Holy Son, a part of Himself! History records His story.[15]

God's "Mystery" is Explained

First He offered them a righteous Law. They rebelled. Then He offered them adoption as His chosen people. The fled to idol-worship. In desperation He sent His only Son to reveal His long-suffering love. They slayed Him on a cross. God snatched Him from the tomb and set Him on a Throne as The Mediator. He offered to His lost children the only remaining way to escape the automatic punishment in Hell; namely, reconciliation, mercy, and grace available through repentance of sin and acceptance of Yeshua's (Jesus') sacrificial gift of Eternal Life.[16]

Now He is telling the world, "Behold, I come quickly!" He is coming for the Body of Believers first; then He must punish a willfully evil world society so that He can establish a righteous rule. From Jerusalem's Throne His blessings will flow to all the earth. No other "god" exists to salvage mankind. None other loves us, nor can! None other has received worse attention from people who were created by their very nature to worship Jehovah.

God's plan was always to offer a series of loving gifts for His earthly *families* to enjoy. They would be His pleasure and His treasure.[17]

Satan's plan of hate was always a series of demonic attacks upon anything which God created or commanded.

Today these final spiritual battle lines are being drawn. Every demon force is being harnessed *on* earth, *in* heaven, and *from* hell. Every human life hangs in the balance awaiting its choice as to which side to join. The results are eternal.[18]

Today's Science Confirms An "End Time"

Scientists are increasingly aware that their varied research projects into outer or inner space reveal a greater Intelligence at work! Findings align with Biblical claims and prophesies with "discomforting" frequency. They admit that "human existence" as we know it has become an endangered species. Mankind has abused or polluted the biology, the ecology, and the sociology of His only world system. Suddenly the pollution at every level from minds to minerals, from air currents to airwaves, from marriages to ministries, confirms the end of our times as being again "as in the days of Noah." Man has converted God's blessings into terminal blights by rejecting His Eternal Light![19]

Today, in every way, Yahweh is trying to say:

"Choose ye this day...."
"There is yet a little while, very little!"[20]

No longer does a thoughtful person disagree with God's Word. Only the "reprobate minds" (beyond any reasoning abilities) rebel against the obvious truths in His Book and rail against His followers whom they label "fools." God's continuing request is that men trust Him whether they can "understand Him" (as "scientists " demand) or just need His Fatherly Hand as does a child in any family. God's mercy and grace invites His adopted and chosen children to watch for Yeshua's soon-coming, while trusting Abba, our Father, for our "daily Bread" and protection![21]

END NOTES

1. John 2:11 **2.** Prov. 16:9 **3.** Luke 10:8-9; I Pet. 2:24; Jer. 23:9 **4.** John 14:26 **5.** James 5:16; Prov. 15:8 **6.** Ps. 119:105 **7.** Matt. 10:20 **8.** John 16:22 **9.** Mark 1:2-4; Rev. 22:20 **10.** Prov. 20:12; Matt. 17:5-6; Luke 21:27 **11.** Rom. 12:3-8; Ps. 40:1-2; Prov. 20:24 **12.** Isa. 42:16; Isa. 43:9-13: Zech. 12:3-9; Mal. 4:1; Zeph. 1:14-18; Rev. 1:10 **13.** Matt. 24:21,30 **14.** Rev. 22:20; Luke 21:28 **15.** Hos. 6:1-3; Rom. 11:25-29; Jer. 31:1; Rom. 8:38; John 3:14-17 **16.** Josh. 8:34; Jer. 5:23-25; Hos. 3:23; Jer. 25:4-6; Jer. 29:11-14; Heb. 1:1-3; Heb. 2:1-4; Heb. 8:8-13; Col. 1:20-22 **17.** Rev. 22:20; Zech. 14:1-9; I John 3:1-3; Rev. 4:11; Ps. 135:4 **18.** II Cor. 10:4; Eph. 6:10-17 **19.** Rom. 1:21-32; II Pet. 3:10-12; Gen 6:5-7; Matt. 25:35-39 **20.** John 12:35;16:16 **21.** Rom. 1:28-32; I Cor. 4:9-10; Ps. 57:1; Rom. 8:14,17

Question #22

"WHAT DOES THE BOOK SAY TO DADS?"

Since our Heavenly Father created His children in His own image, I was certain that His Book would contain advice to His earthly dads who procreate (that is, beget on behalf of Him). It does. The loving nature of our Father in Heaven saturates His Book with directions for successful living and loving as husbands and dads. At this late date in human history, the evidence is piled high and deep that only *His* statutes can withstand the stresses of modern family pressures.[1]

His guidelines are really simple prescriptions for making God's promises come true that "this is the day that the Lord hath made!" Some of God's principles for conduct in "running the affairs of a family" are listed below:[2]

Heavenly Helps for Happy Homes

1. God ordained that a father should be the head of a family unit. As its leader, his authority is to be exercised after appropriate appraisal and consideration of the unit's needs. Otherwise, his actions will prove counter-productive. He is the "priest" of the family that God has given him to shepherd: he is the appointed caretaker as head of his family.[3]

2. The father is to respect, cherish and co-labor with his wife and children as they function and grow and serve one another. Mom is his objective adviser, and the children are the proofs of their combined labors. Final decisions become Dad's responsibility after prayerful evaluation. Loving discipline leads to living learning![4]

3. Family "rights" can only emerge from properly assumed responsibilities. Father must assume charge, using head and heart with love and justice for all. Children's "rights" grow in response to their own obedience and respect for guidance. Dad must clarify "loose ends." After all, it says so in The BOOK![5]

4. *Financial matters* involve each family member at some level. God has stated, and has proved, that He is Provider of the Family of God. The earthly father is responsible to the Heavenly Father, while the mother acts as the co-partner in that stewardship. Prayer for financial "prosperity" must be balanced by prudent moderation else the prayer becomes farcical lust or grim greed. God can not break His own command! His children must "first seek the Kingdom of Heaven." Only then can material blessings be continued by the Giver of all good things.[6]

5. Since *family frictions* arise from misunderstandings fanned by selfishness, "Dad," as the family priest, must assume charge by dousing the flames with love, fairness, firmness, and with "hand-holding prayer." The family's ground rules are re-explained and thoughtfully upgraded to befit accountability, emerging talents, and growing responsibilities. Dad explains that the "rights" of each family member are determined by performance in "little things"; rewards are permits to enjoy "greater things." Self-discipline always speeds the growth.[7]

6. The father of a *growing family* must be creative in providing times, places, and events for growth to occur. Home is not merely a place to hide out with a TV or racing form, but a stage for sharing precious moments with Mom and kids. Each day must be regarded as a page from a thickening family album of individual deeds and dreams, trials and triumphs, flavored with cooperation and compassion. Dad must share himself with Mom and kids, proudly attentive to daily needs and deeds. God outlines His winning program that way because it works and it can be done.[8]

7. Above all, dads owe themselves a victory by keeping their own "act" clean, thinking on those things which elevate, while holding tight to the Heavenly Hand and walking in the stillness of God's Garden with an attentive ear![9]

Dads Are God's Assigned Helpers

A loving dad reflects the devotion, protection, and providence which typify his Heavenly Father's care. Dad listens to his Heavenly Abba Who speaks through His Comforter, through His written contracts (the ancient Torah and Scrolls) and through His "better covenant" (the Good News Gospel and Letters)! Dad, as family priest, must convey to his entrusted family these everlasting truths and promises from Elohim, the El Shaddai, the Yeshua, the Messiah, the Adonai, the God of All creation![10]

Having heeded and followed Jehovah's instructions, Dad can enjoy the unsearchable riches of his daily walk with the only Most High God. With his ear tuned, he will hear the soon-sounding triumphant blast from the final shofar-trumpet signalling God's victory over unrighteousness. Dad can clasp his lovely family to his breast as they leap to meet the everlasting Messiah Whose Glory wipes away all tears![11]

HALLELUJAH

"Old things are passed away;
Behold, all things are become new...[12]

Wherefore, come out from among them, and be ye separate, saith the LORD, and touch not the unclean things; and I will receive you, and will be a Father unto you, and ye shall be my sons and daughters, saith the LORD ALMIGHTY."[13]

Amazing as it is, the BOOK reveals Jehovah's consuming need for a human family to share His love for them and with them! He has literally gone beyond His "call of duty" to tell human dads and moms and all "little children" to seek the Father's Kingdom first. Then He can add His daily blessings. It is up to dads to point his family to Yeshua, their *daily* Bread.[14]

END NOTES

1. Jer. 31:1; Ps. 40:5-9; Deut. 6:6-7; Gal. 5:14;22-23; Ps. 19:7-9; Ps. 37:30-31 **2.** Ps. 118:24 **3.** I Pet. 2:5; Ps. 127:3; Prov. 22:6; Col. 3:21; Eph. 6:4 **4.** Luke 15:20; I Pet. 3:7; Titus 2:5; Isa. 28:9 **5.** Eph. 5:25,28; Prov. 19:18; Eph. 6:1-3; Prov. 3:12 **6.** II Cor. 12:14; Luke 12:15; James 4:2-3; Rev. 3:17: Matt. 6:33 **7.** I Sam. 8:3; Deut. 6:7; Prov. 29:15; Mark 10:9; Prov. 19:13; Luke 19:17 **8.** Eccles. 9:9; Mal. 3:16 **9.** Col. 3:2-6; Phil. 4:8-9; Matt. 7:11 **10.** Rom. 8:15-17; Heb. 8:6-13; Heb. 10:16-18; Isa. 40:25-31 **11.** Rom. 11:33; Dan. 3:26; I Cor. 15:52; Deut. 6:24-25; Isa. 25:8-9 **12.** II Cor. 5:17 **13.** II Cor. 6:17-18 **14.** Eph. 3:14-15; Jer. 24:7; Isa. 45:17-19; Isa. 46:9,12-13; Luke 12:29-32; John 6:35

CONCLUSION

"Didn't You Read My Book?"

Yeshua's question remains uppermost as His advice for today! Like His spoken Word the Written Word reveals ALL that His earthly children need to know about His purposes for them and their need of Him. He says so in His Scriptures. He also said so to me when He snatched me into Paradise and later met me in Lazarus' Tomb: "I must show you things and tell you others, so that you can go tell them, tell them, tell them!" His Voice was that of a silver trumpet when He was speaking to me those words. It changed my goals in life, just as His words, written or spoken, can change lives anywhere.[1]

The urgency of *"searching Scriptures"* is overwhelming. Jehovah's offer of a free gift of Eternal Life starting now during His Age of *mercy and grace, will expire soon!* His Book also foretells a *soon return* of His Lamb (our Shepherd). It *foretells* that "it is given unto man once to die, and then the judgment." His Book reveals a Righteous Supreme God Whose justice requires His purging the world of all sin. His Mercy, however, is so *great* that He has offered His rebellious human beings (originally created to be a righteous family for *His* pleasure) total *reconciliation* with Him *NOW* through faith and trust in

His Son Yeshua. The only option God can offer human rebels is to "perish."[2]

As we read His Book we are *alerted* to the exact methods and results which the Supreme God of the universe must use to punish and purge His "so-loved-earth" of the *blackness of human sin*! (The time is soon.) Yeshua foresaw it as the *worst* tribulation in all of history. The immensity of *God's wrath* against Satan, demons, and their human followers *is awesome*, as recorded in the Written Word. God has called it *The Day Of The Lord*, a Day of Wrath, a Time of Jacob's Trouble, a holocaust when evil men will hide in caves and cry out for them to collapse upon them to end their terror. Heat will destroy crops, and cannibalism will follow. *Evil* will be a *life-style* to the extent that men will still curse God rather than deny the "deity" of Satan or themselves![3]

Forever Loving

Our God of Love has always *offered* His alternative plan to any and all of His creatures. *Without* their works but *with* their will-power, He suggests (but never coerces) that they "choose this day whom you will serve." He even offers to do everything necessary to change them from self-righteous *losers* to righteous *winners* (in Jesus)! He even provides the *measure* of faith, Jesus' cleansing *blood*, the gift of *eternal* life, and a *new* mind and heart to enjoy His "abundant life" *right now* on earth! *HE* writes our names in His Book of Life (NOT a book of wrath) once we return His love through our worship.[4]

Everlasting Promises

His Book contains so many *promises* for "His children of righteousness" that it has required sixty-six books in two Testaments of thousands of chapters just to record the plans, purposes, and promises which He has laid out for the human family in His BIBLE, His only official textbook.[5]

If any readers of this little book (a testimony of Jesus' touch upon my life) have not yet thrilled at the excitement of letting God guide your life, invite Him in *today*. Join the family of believers who have "reasoned together" and have *accepted* a newness of life with Jehovah-God as The Heavenly Father, Yeshua as your Savior/Mediator, and the Holy Spirit of God as an Indweller/Teacher![6]

YESHUA Himself offers this divine advice:

"ASK and it shall be given unto you;
"SEEK and ye shall find;
"KNOCK and it shall be opened unto you!"[7]

HIS BOOK poses this vital question for each to answer:

"HOW SHALL WE ESCAPE IF WE NEGLECT SO GREAT A SALVATION?"[8]

God's Grand Final Question

The BOOK promises that Messiah is *soon* returning in His resurrection body: first in the Cloud to collect His believers together as His Body of which He is the Head, and later to Jerusalem as the King of Kings upon David's eternal throne to establish a righteous rule in the world under His Heavenly Father.[9]

The BOOK gives all the necessary guides for us to *escape* from spiritual darkness and death, and to *emerge* into the light of God's love and presence now.[10]

That is why Messiah is asking His created children of every age, nation or color, whether Jew or Gentile, men or women, chained or free, saved or lost.[11]

"DIDN'T YOU READ MY BOOK?"

END NOTES

1. II Tim. 3:14-17; II Tim. 2:15; Prov. 2:1 to 3:26; Rev. 1:10; Rev. 4:1 **2.** John 5:39,46-47; Isa. 26:16-20: Isa. 49:1; Matt. 11:13-15; Matt. 12:36; Isa. 28:18,22; Heb. 1:1-3; Rom. 9:22-24; Ps. 136; Rev. 4:11; Eph. 1:5; II Cor. 5:18-19; John 3:16 **3.** Zeph. 1:14-18; Dan. 12:1-4; I John 1:6; I John 2:15-17; Matt. 24:21; Zeph. 1:14-18; Rev. 6:15-17; Rev. 16:9; Deut. 58:53-57; Rev. 9:6,20-21 **4.** I John 3:1-2; Josh. 24:15; I John 3:7,10; Rom. 12:3 **5.** I John 2:29; II Cor. 5:21; Hosea 10:12; Rev. 22:18-19 **6.** Rev. 3:20-22; Isa. 1:18; Rev. 22:16-17 **7.** Luke 11:9-10 **8.** Heb. 2:3 **9.** Rev. 22:7,10,12,20; I Cor. 15:51-57; Zech. 6:12-13; Luke 1:32-33; Isa. 65:17-19; John. 13:34-35; Dan. 7:13-14 **10.** John 1:4-5; John 12:46-50 **11.** Gal. 3:28-29

IN MEMORIAM

To my wife, Maybelle, whom Jesus took home after loaning her to me for seven sevens of wonderful years together:

And

To my precious son and daughter whom she bore and reared in the love of God while making our home a sanctuary and our community a better place for our friends;

This little book of remembrances is gratefully dedicated as we all await the triumphant trumpet's sound to learn more about our Joyous Jesus, the Loving Lord, Who has made possible our lives here and hereafter.

Maybelle O. Eby

POSTSCRIPT

"LAND OF BEGINNING AGAIN"

Note: Just as this book's manuscript was nearing comple-tion, so was Maybelle's earthly life span. Her seemingly limit-less love for family, friends, and God's calling to serve wherever there was a need suddenly completed her role on earth. One morning her Lord called her home into His Glory, as she whispered a tender "Good-bye. I'll see you again soon!" I bent to look into her blind eyes. As she took her final breath, her lids opened and I saw a miracle: in them was reflected the blazing light of Paradise. She had arrived in Yeshua's open arms! Her new life of divine health had begun. Inwardly, I shouted: "Thank you, Jesus, for healing her this day!"

On a lonely restless day, in my empty house, I penned a note to my Heavenly Father, listing eight qualifications which would be essential for a new helpmate (in my opinion) to live with me till the Rapture! I explained that I had neither time to seek nor wisdom to choose, but He had both. I added, "If you have been preparing such a remarkable lady, let us find each other soon!" I laid the note on my bedspread, and further reminded Him verbally: "Lord, You learned to read long before I learned to write. Furthermore, You made the Hebrew custom that the father was to choose a bride for His son! Thank you for Your promises to supply my needs!" He went to work.

In Barbara's Words

"There is a Land of Beginning Again, and GOD in His great, merciful, Divine, farsighted, wise and understanding

Love-Plan ordained that the dream of a 70 year-old lady and the desire of a 76 year-old gentleman be miraculously fulfilled by joining these two ships that had passed in the night, times without number, only to be directed to the same lighthouse—destined for the same harbor!

"First a letter—then on August 9, 1987, our first meeting—then months later a message (from God to Dick in the night): 'Go get her; I prepared you for each other!' And one year to the day after the first meeting a joining of hearts and hands with one hope and one habitat!

"Barbara, whose name means 'stranger,' is just that in essence. She was born an only child, saved from a deathbed by a miracle when a year old, called by God in dreams and visions at age ten. She traveled as a musician in His service from age thirteen, and from thence living a life led by her Lord encompassing 70 years of 'wandering in the wilderness' with scars of solitary soldiering, all for the purposed preparation for receiving the desire of her heart, and fulfilling the faith of her fathers. Beaten into the dust from whence she came—hence birthing 'beauty for ashes'— a meaning and hope became life for her favorite Scripture: 'And they shall take away the ashes from the Altar and spread a purple cloth thereon' (Numbers 4:13).

"Immediately following the wedding, as pre-scheduled months before, we flew to Eden Prairie, Minnesota, to speak in Roger Davis' Church of The Jubilee. Without a honeymoon this was both fulfilling and rewarding. One year later, on our first Anniversary, we received this beautiful painting by his everloving wife, Marlene. It is our most prized painting depicting our 'Land of Beginning Again.' As such we gratefully share it with you."

Barbara B. Eby

Richard E. Eby, D.O., D.Sc. (Hon), D.Ed .(Hon), Ph. D. (Hon) F.A.C.O.O.G.

Who is Dr. Eby? Well known in his profession as an OB/Gyn Doctor and Professor at the California College of Osteopathic Physicians and Surgeons, he became active in academic affairs, serving as President of the American College of Osteopathic OB/GYN, President of the Kansas City College of Osteopathy and Surgery, Executive Assistant at the American Osteopathic Assn., Professor of OB/GYN at Kirksville College, co-founder of Park Ave. Hospital, College of Osteopathic Medicine of the Pacific, and charter President of the Osteopathic Physicians and Surgeons of California in 1961.

When the Lord called him into a full-time ministry in 1978 Dr. Eby closed his medical office in order to "Go tell them, tell them" wherever the Holy Spirit might lead. He is now proclaiming the Good News of God's love, His healing, and His soon return wherever TV, radio, or audiences request his unusual testimony. he has authored three previous books:

CAUGHT UP INTO PARADISE
TELL THEM I AM COMING
THE AMAZING LAMB OF GOD

This latest book includes Scripture references to events and miracles which parallel his "last generation" experiences as a follower of God's Yeshua, the Jesus of Nazareth.